Praise for *Wicca Made Easy*

'Wicca Made Easy *is pure magic. I was enchanted from the very page. Phyllis Curott has articulated the ancient language and practice of Divinity known as Wicca that speaks to our very bone marrow and welcomes us home to the Sacredness of everyday life.'*

CHRISTIANE NORTHRUP, M.D., NEW YORK TIMES BEST-SELLING AUTHOR OF *GODDESSES NEVER AGE* AND *WOMEN'S BODIES, WOMEN'S WISDOM*

'In this lively and engaging introduction to the rebirth of an ancient wisdom way, Phyllis Curott invites us to embrace the whole of creation as imbued with the sacred and our own bodies as boundlessly holy. This book is a call to community, an endorsement of feminine leadership, a remembrance of our birthright of mutual belonging and beautiful magic.'

MIRABAI STARR, AUTHOR OF *GOD OF LOVE* AND *CARAVAN OF NO DESPAIR*

'Wicca offers spiritual wisdom and wholeness that have been missing in the popular culture for millennia. Phyllis Curott takes us beyond the erroneous beliefs of a patriarchal past by embracing the Goddess and bringing forth passion, truth and healing with nature, and for all. Her gem of a book restores Wicca's potent do-able rituals in everyday practice. In co-creating with Mother Nature we can erase habits cemented by misguided history and reclaim inner harmony, grace and gratitude.'

MAYA TIWARI, AYURVEDA AUTHOR, HUMANITARIAN AND PEACE LEADER

'Bringing the Old Religion in tune with the modern spirits of Nature, this book is a must for anyone exploring the Craft and its more shamanic aspects and incorporating them into modern Witchcraft practice.'

JANET FARRAR AND GAVIN BONE, AUTHORS OF *A WITCHES' BIBLE, THE WITCHES' GODDESS, THE INNER MYSTERIES* AND *LIFTING THE VEIL*

'In this fresh and evolved book for newcomers as well as adepts, Phyllis shares her wisdom and life experience with writing that is cohesive, smooth and anchored in a relaxed and welcoming tone. Clear, enlightened – both energetically and practically – and really well organized in the way the wisdom and practices unfold. I love the strong shamanic wisdom shining through.'

FIONA HORNE, AUTHOR OF POP! GOES THE WITCH AND THE NAKED WITCH

'A much-needed guide in a time when humanity needs to re-learn the sacredness of all life. These pages will tune you in to the divinity within you and also the divinity within all sacred creation. A great little book for the merely curious as well as for those who want to delve deeper.'

ELLEN EVERT HOPMAN, AUTHOR OF THE REAL WITCHES OF NEW ENGLAND, SECRET MEDICINES FROM YOUR GARDEN AND A LEGACY OF DRUIDS

'Phyllis Curott weaves the Wiccan revival together with core shamanism, and this welcomed book provides an accessible guide for blossoming intuition into an awakened personal magic, awareness and purpose. With refreshing clarity, she conveys for people of all genders the appeal of a modern witchcraft that is capable of serving a world in need of a sanely organic and joyful re-balancing.'

PROFESSOR MICHAEL YORK, BATH SPA UNIVERSITY, CONTRIBUTOR TO PAGAN ETHICS

'Wicca Made Easy covers the many mysteries of Wiccan theory and practice and reveals itself as far more of an active workbook than a typical reference. Covering the fundamentals with a keen insight honed from years of practice, Phyllis pleasantly places Nature and its beauty in the forefront of her mystical practices. Wicca Made Easy would be a perfect gift for a new initiate eager to begin experiencing Nature's powerful and spiritual scope and all things magical.

ANDREW THEITIC, PUBLISHER OF THE WITCHES' ALMANAC AND CO-AUTHOR OF THE REDE OF THE WICCAE

WICCA

Made Easy

Also in the *Made Easy* series

WICCA

Made Easy

AWAKEN THE DIVINE
MAGIC WITHIN YOU

PHYLLIS CUROTT

Bestselling author of *Book of Shadows*

HAY HOUSE

Carlsbad, California • New York City
London • Sydney • New Delhi

Published in the United Kingdom by:
Hay House UK Ltd, The Sixth Floor, Watson House
54 Baker Street, London W1U 7BU
Tel: +44 (0)20 3927 7290; Fax: +44 (0)20
3927 7291; www.hayhouse.co.uk

Published in the United States of America by:
Hay House Inc., PO Box 5100, Carlsbad, CA 92018-5100
Tel: (1) 760 431 7695 or (800) 654 5126
Fax: (1) 760 431 6948 or (800) 650 5115
www.hayhouse.com

Published in Australia by:
Hay House Australia Ltd, 18/36 Ralph St, Alexandria NSW 2015
Tel: (61) 2 9669 4299; Fax: (61) 2 9669 4144
www.hayhouse.com.au

Published in India by:
Hay House Publishers India, Muskaan Complex, Plot No.3, B-2,
Vasant Kunj, New Delhi 110 070
Tel: (91) 11 4176 1620; Fax: (91) 11 4176 1630
www.hayhouse.co.in

A catalogue record for this book is available from the British Library.

Tradepaper ISBN: 978-1-78817-163-2
E-book ISBN: 978-1-78817-172-4
11 10 9 8 7 6 5 4 3

Interior illustrations: 102, 162 Liron Gilenberg | www.ironicitalics.com

Printed in the United States of America

Contents

List of Practices

Introduction

'I feel like I've come home.'

*We're all on a journey, pilgrims seeking our power,
our purpose and our higher selves. We're looking
for inner peace and outer prosperity, the courage
to face our fears and fulfill our destiny, to leave
loneliness behind and find love, to change the way
we think and the way we live. We're looking for Spirit
and for guidance in our quest for wholeness. We're
looking to awaken the magic within.*

*Life is complicated, but your spirituality shouldn't be.
Life is also magical, and your spirituality should be.*

When I discovered Wicca almost 40 years ago, there
were just a few hundred people in the back of a dusty
old broom closet, reviving an ancestral wisdom tradition
hidden from the world after hundreds of years of
persecution and negative stereotypes. Today, there are

more than one million public Wiccans in the USA, and Wicca has become the fastest-growing spirituality in the British Isles, Europe and Australia and is expanding throughout the world.

The birth of a new religion is rare and the rebirth of one of the most ancient is remarkable. It's an awakening from dreams of divinity that no longer fit the world we live in or the spiritual longings we have. Many are drawn to Wicca because it offers spiritual wisdom and wholeness that have been missing for millennia, welcoming the return of the Goddess, the rising Feminine, and honoring women as spiritual leaders.

At a critical time of mounting environmental devastation, Wicca reveres Mother Earth as an embodiment of divinity. And in a sophisticated, educated, global culture marked by a decline in traditional religious adherence, Wicca is non-dogmatic and non-hierarchical. It's a deeply personal spiritual practice that anyone can master to experience divinity. And you don't have to be Wiccan to benefit from its wisdom or its practices, just as you don't have to be Hindu to benefit from yoga or Buddhist to practice meditation.

Practicing Wicca helped me to take off a blindfold, tied on by history and habit, that I hadn't realized I'd been wearing. I saw realms of Spirit I'd never known existed. I saw the world I lived in every day as it really is – *sacred*. And I began to see that I too was sacred. Wicca awakened the divine magic within me and opened me to the divine magic in the world all around me.

A bit of my story

I discovered Wicca when I couldn't have been less interested in anything spiritual. And I certainly didn't believe in magic! I'd gotten my BA in philosophy from an Ivy League school in the USA, my Juris Doctor from a top law school, and had just begun practicing law, fighting organized crime in trade unions. I didn't expect the world to be paradise, let alone magical, but I did expect to do my part to make it a better place.

That's how I'd been raised: in an intellectual, humanist family with parents whose lives had been devoted to social justice. Rather than a particular religion, they taught me to believe in the goodness of the human heart and to live by the Golden Rule: treat others the way I wanted to be treated. That was enough for me. Until my second year in law school...

I began having premonitions that manifested and intuitions that proved true. I knew the phone would ring before it did and who was calling. I knew answers in class without having read the cases. My senses were heightened and, for a while, I had a photographic memory, which, you can imagine, was *very* helpful for passing the Bar Exam. Most tantalizing of all was a sense of... presence, as if the world was actually alive and aware. There was also a recurring dream of a woman, seated, a crown on her head, a book in her lap and a soft light glowing above her heart.

I had no framework to understand what was going on. I'd practiced yoga since high school, but I'd been too young for the psychedelic 60s and I lived in New York, not California. Ever the rationalist, I started reading books on quantum physics, then books on the extraordinary connections between quantum physics and consciousness. I learned that there was more to reality than I'd been taught in school. But nothing I read explained *why* it was happening.

Still, I trusted what I was experiencing. I allowed the possibility that there was reality beyond the limits of what I was supposed to believe and achieve. And so I was led, by dreams and events, signs and synchronicities, and a friend who called herself a White Witch, to the least likely, most unimaginable encounter in the world: behind a hidden door in the back of a dusty old bookstore called *The Magickal Childe*, with a group of women practicing Wicca.

A group of Witches, practicing Witchcraft.

I was invited to join them. It was the last thing in the world I was interested in. After all, they were *Witches*. In other words, weird. Very weird. I politely declined. Life went on as before but the dreams and intuitions and alive-ness evaporated. I was going numb; I was returning to 'normal.' And then the woman in my dream reappeared.

I was wandering around the Metropolitan Museum of Art, trying to figure out my next career move, when she appeared exactly as she had in my dream: seated as still as the stone she was carved from. The world filled with light and a guard had to help me sit down. When I recovered I read the shining brass plaque beside her: *The Libyan Sibyl*. Back home, I looked up the word sibyl: 'An ancient prophetess or Witch.' I accepted the invitation.

It *was* weird. A room full of women stood in a circle gesticulating at the four directions, saying things I didn't understand, passing round a silver goblet filled with... grape juice, and talking about the Goddess. But they were smart and interesting, and diverse in age, race and background; some were gay, others were straight. Each week I was invited to return, and I did. Gradually, what they were doing and why they were doing it became clear.

I read about the European Witchcraze, the Burning Times – a persecution of almost 500 years during which more than 100,000 women, some men and even children, were accused, tortured and hideously murdered for practicing the 'Old Religion.' I began to realize that my ideas about Witchcraft were negative stereotypes from fairy tales, movies and Halloween decorations – all influenced by the Witchcraze – that had nothing to do with what these women actually believed or practiced. I learned that *Wicca* is a very old English word that's the root of the word *Witch*, and that both words meant a wise one, someone who sees the Sacred.

I started seeing. I saw the beautiful face of the Goddess behind the mask of the hideous hag, and discovered the Witch was the figure onto whom patriarchy projected its fears of women, their power and sexuality. The modern Witch is, just like the Goddess she reveres, the ultimate feminist icon. As a young lawyer dealing every day with sexual harassment and discrimination, that worked for me.

The revelations were liberating and empowering. And then, magical. I finally *saw* the Goddess. She appeared as we cast our circles, shining within each of the women. I saw Artemis's strength and courage, Lakshmi's sensuality, Brigid's healing poetry, Athena's wisdom, Ceres's maternal love and generosity, Morrigan's warrior power, Pele's fire and Hecate's dark mysteries.

In the mirror of the Goddess, I began to see a spark of that Divine Feminine energy within myself. I understood that our bodies are sacred, our intuition a gift and our wisdom invaluable. Deity was no longer an old, white, unavailable male on the other side of the clouds, passing judgment on us. The Goddess was alive, present and restoring wholeness to divinity. And at each Sabbat – the eight seasonal holy days honoring Nature's divine wisdom – when men came to celebrate with us, I discovered a different kind of God present in the world, dancing, loving and in partnership with the Goddess.

It was radical. It was revolutionary. Most of all, it was *real*. I didn't *believe* in the Goddess or the God. I *experienced them*. Wicca wasn't a belief system *about* divinity. It was a spiritual practice providing experiences *of* divinity. The ground I was standing on shifted once again. It became sacred.

And it wasn't complicated. Wicca didn't require me to suspend my rational disbelief, or to master long, strange magical incantations, or lists of odd ingredients. It was simple, it was joyful and it was natural. It felt like remembering something that I already knew. And best of all, it worked. The magic within me was awakening, and as it did I began to experience the divine magic in the world around me.

The presence I'd sensed when my adventure began reappeared right before my very eyes. Even though I lived in the midst of one of the world's greatest cities, I saw that the natural world *embodied* divinity. The Air was breath, Fire spirit, Water blood, and Earth body. Wiccan practices helped me attune myself – mind, body and spirit – and come into harmony with Nature, with the elements, the seasonal cycles and with the Moon, whose rhythm and spiritual wisdom belonged to women. I saw that love is a force of Nature and that we are all children of Mother Earth, regardless of our religion.

My intuition blossomed and developed into a higher awareness. I began to discern a greater purpose for my life and achieving all that I wanted from it became easier. Divine magic happened as the Sacred manifested in my life. I learned to *make* magic,' to alter my consciousness, set intentions, invoke Goddess and God, raise and receive energy, cast spells and offer thanks and rejoice in the blessings bestowed and the magic that manifested. It was like the Law of Attraction on steroids.

At the same time, I began practicing core shamanism with the now famous Brooklyn Group. Developed by Dr. Michael Harner, the work focused on the essential practices of the world's oldest spiritual tradition shared by most Indigenous cultures throughout history and across the globe. The world expanded further into realms of Spirit and I was accompanied and guided by spirit allies and power animals. What I learned 'there' had profound value for me 'here,' and I recognized the shamanic roots of modern Wicca, transforming how and why I practice it.

I was initiated – the story I tell in my first memoir, *Book of Shadows* – and became a Wiccan High Priestess. I was the first Priestess to weave Wicca and core shamanism together as an integral sacred technology and, after 20 years, my teaching was formalized as the Tradition of Ara, the Latin word for altar, the point at the center of Creation where Spirit and Earth are One.

I refused to be limited by negative stereotypes – as a Wiccan, a Witch or a woman – and was one of the first American Wiccan Priestesses to 'come out of the broom closet.' I handled or consulted on groundbreaking cases establishing the legal rights of Wiccans and was an advocate in global media campaigns challenging the negative stereotypes.

I won't say it was easy. I lost some clients and friends, faced betrayals and sorrows, and grieved when I couldn't have children. I faced my self-doubt and lack of confidence and struggled with depression and despair as I felt the suffering of others and Mother Earth as my own. I came to understand that we're shaped by blessings *and* by challenges. Real magic happens when we transform our wounds into wellbeing, losses into new life, darkness into illumination. What I gained far surpassed anything I'd lost or sacrificed.

I created a successful law practice, wrote internationally bestselling books that made Wicca accessible to the world and helped thousands discover the divine magic of the world they live in and that lives within them. In the USA, *Jane Magazine* honored me as 'One of the Ten Gutsiest Women of the Year.' I was twice elected the first Wiccan Vice Chair of the Parliament of the World's Religions and created its historic 2015 Inaugural Women's Assembly. I received other acknowledgements of spiritual and cultural ground breaking, but the greatest honor was my induction into the Martin Luther King Jr. Collegium of Clergy and Scholars.

And then, at the height of this rebellious, impossible success, I released it all. I went into the wilderness, leaving behind all that I'd accomplished and everything I thought I knew. I went in search of the Mystery. It found me, appearing as the Green Man in the center of a labyrinth in Italy and leading me on a quest across the globe and home again. There, in my backyard, I was shown that Nature's laws are spiritual laws, that each individual life works by making all Life better and that love really is the source of Creation. I reawakened to the divine magic of the natural world, and within myself.

My journey has been unique and deeply magical, but it's always struck me that if I, a skeptical New York lawyer, could have such extraordinary experiences and awaken to the magic within myself, anyone could. This book distills the spiritual principles and practices of Wicca – as I have practiced and taught it for almost 40 years – that I hope will open your awareness, connect you to the divinity of the world you're living in and awaken the magic of *you*.

Everyone gets tapped on the shoulder, gets a call from the Sacred to awaken. If reading this sounds like what you've always known, if it feels like this might be that call, or an affirmation of the call you've already received, let me be the first to say: *Welcome to the divine magic within. Welcome home!*

How to Work with This Book

Wicca made Easy is not your typical Wiccan guidebook. It's not a book of recipes and formulas for mechanical spellcasting and instant gratification. *It's a guide to awakening the divine magic within you.*

The key to this book is that it requires your interaction. You can't just read it – you've got to do the practices to awaken your magic. I promise, if you work it, it will work. The practices are presented in an order that will cultivate your spiritual skills and gifts, and they can be used by you alone, or with a study group or even a coven, moving at your own pace.

Your magical journal

As you work with this book, you're going to keep a magical journal. In it, I'll ask you to write about your experiences and encounters, reflections and revelations, dreams and journeys, intuitions and synchronicities and the spells and rituals you create. And of course, you should feel free to write in it whenever you're moved to.

Keeping a magical journal will be incredibly useful for remembering what you did, experienced and felt; the insights, epiphanies and inspiration you've had, and for seeing your breakthroughs, growth and progress. Most importantly, it will help you see the patterns and lessons, deities and signs of destiny, the great and sacred story emerging in your life.

Your Book of Shadows

If Wicca speaks to you as a spiritual practice you'd like to pursue, start your own Book of Shadows. I've included a simple guide to this in Chapter 12. Like keeping your journal, it's an incredibly magical, creative and empowering project.

I hope you find this little book opens a world of wonder and divine magic for you. So, let's get started!

Chapter 1

Wise Ones

Wicca is a spiritual path into worlds of wonder. It's a path into your inner world, where real magic begins; a path into the Other World, where spirits live; a path that brings you back home transformed, empowered and able to see the Sacred in the world.

The journey will open your awareness and your heart, heal and reconnect you to the divine context in which you live. The ordinary becomes extraordinary and the extraordinary becomes possible because Creation is divine. That's when magic begins to awaken within you and to manifest all around you.

The roots of Wicca are ancestral, but its revival is perfectly timed and speaks to the very heart of our modern lives and longings, challenges and destiny. Wicca is deeply personal and simultaneously universal. The practices are simple and the results are profound.

Wicca has no holy book, no prophet or institution dictating what to believe or how to practice. There's no single definition, no One True Way. Wicca honors and encourages individual approaches, experiences and conclusions. Throughout our journey together, I encourage you to trust your intuition, your feelings, your experiences, as you find *your* way – the way that works for you.

Wicca is a path of personal spiritual practice, responsibility and revelation. But you're not alone. Though each of us has our own unique path, we're all traveling in the same sacred landscape, and there's always a teacher, a guide, a spirit along the way. In the midst of extraordinary individuality and diversity, there are essential spiritual practices and principles that we all seem to share. We have similar experiences, celebrate the same seasonal holy days (Sabbats) and lunar rhythms (Esbats), and ultimately, we come to remarkably similar insights about divinity, Nature and human nature. There's an essential sacred wisdom we share and that we call Wicca.

A brief look at Wicca's fascinating history

To really understand contemporary Wicca, its wisdom and practices, what you'll be doing and why, it's important to understand where it comes from. There's been no small effort and controversy in understanding Wicca's origins and evolution. All religions have myths about their beginnings, but in the case of Wicca, the reality is more fascinating than the myth. There are reasons that Wicca is called the Craft of the Wise.

Roots

The word itself is a great place to start. Wicca arrived in Britain with the Anglo-Saxons in the mid-5th century, but it was already a lot older. Its roots go back some 5,500 years, to the most widely spoken language in the world, called Proto-Indo-European, and the word *weid*. *Weid* means 'to see' or 'to know,' and it's also the root of the Old English *wisean,* 'to make wise or knowing.' There are also roots to divination, or speaking with divinity. Originally, *wicca* was male and *wicce* female. Now we use Wiccan (capitalized) as a non-gender specific term and Wicca to refer to the spirituality.

How did Wicca get connected to Witch? Simple: the pronunciation of *wicce* is *witch-a* and in the 16th century, the Modern English spelling became *witch*. But the origin of both words provides a very different portrait from the negative stereotype of the evil, Satan-worshipping hag, and reminds us that there were Indigenous traditions in England, and in fact, throughout Europe and the Fertile Crescent (the Middle East), long before the arrival of Christianity and the vicious stereotype.

A Wiccan is a wise one who knows and sees the Sacred. Until a few hundred years ago, Wiccans were a village's shamans.

Wicca and shamanism

Wicca is rooted in shamanism, humanity's oldest spirituality. Some call it the Old Religion. Today shamanism is still practiced throughout the world by around 370 million Indigenous (First, Native or Aboriginal) peoples, despite centuries of brutal colonial domination.

We don't often think of Europe as having Indigenous peoples, yet the majority of Europe's inhabitants are considered to be Indigenous; however, the contemporary practice of ancestral traditions – as seen with the Sami people of northern Scandinavia and the Basque of northern Spain and southern France – is rare. Modern Wiccans and others are just now rediscovering, reviving and reconstructing the traditions of their Indigenous forebears.

And a modern form of core shamanism, composed of essential practices common to many shamanic traditions but without specific cultural overlays, is being increasingly practiced by the modern descendants of immigrants from Europe, Russia, Africa and elsewhere who are also rediscovering their Indigenous ancestral traditions.

All over the world, shamans serve similar roles. S/he is the village's healer, the midwife of babies, lost souls and souls that have passed, the conductor of ceremony, celebration and rites of passage. S/he is the interpreter of dreams and signs, the journeyer between worlds, the keeper and revealer of Mysteries. Shamans travel backward and forward in time, between Spirit realms and back home again, bringing healing and help for themselves, others and the world. Shamanic wisdom traditions are deeply connected to the Earth, to the place where people live, to the spirit of place – the *genius loci* in Latin – and especially to the spirit of wild places where people do not live.

Everything has a spirit, and shamans work with the spirits of Air, Fire, Water and especially Mother Earth. They know that all beings are related, that animals are teachers, plants are healers and helpers, and there are guardian spirits, power animals, spirit helpers, ancestors and allies who will assist us.

If there's one central wisdom at the heart of shamanism, and Wicca, it is that all of life is sacred. There's one common reality with no separation between Spirit and Nature, divinity and humanity, humanity and Nature. All is connected, all is One.

Shamans are masters of balancing, harmonizing and uniting inner and outer, the visible and invisible, the Spirit and the world. Across the globe, shamans use similar techniques to open themselves to the Sacred and to live in harmony with Nature. They shift and open their consciousness with ecstatic practices like drumming, chanting, dancing, journeying, praying, vision-seeking, communion with holy plants, working with natural energies and elements, ritual and ceremony.

Many years ago, when I first began to practice Wicca and core shamanism simultaneously, the ecstatic practices that shifted my perception and enabled me to move into the Other World (non-ordinary reality) were incredibly important and powerful. They changed my understanding of the nature of reality, confirmed experiences I'd had and restored spiritual abilities I didn't know I had. A new dimension, a world of Spirit, opened to me. It changed my life.

As I simultaneously attended my weekly Wiccan circle and my weekly shamanic circle, I recognized the similarities: working in circle, honoring the directions and working with the elements, honoring Mother Earth, Father Sun and the Moon, the seasonal shifts and lunar rhythms – practices that opened my consciousness – and ecstatic practices like dancing and chanting, as well as the offering of thanks and much more.

Over the years, I've come to appreciate that shamans are also seers of the Sacred *in* the world we live in every day, and especially the natural world. At this precarious moment when the future is imperiled because of our blindness to Creation's innate divinity, this may be one of the greatest gifts of shamanism, and Wicca. Though continuity has been broken, especially in Europe, and many traditions and a lot of wisdom has been lost, the essential sources of that wisdom remain. We have the same great spiritual teacher, our Mother Earth, the same essential shamanic practices (core shamanism), the helping spirits, and the same innate ability to experience the Sacred.

Not everyone becomes a shaman, but anyone can practice shamanism. Not everyone becomes a Priest/ess, but anyone can practice Wicca. Yet for hundreds of years, practicing Wicca, practicing Witchcraft or even being accused of being a *wicce* could get you killed.

Rupture

Tragically, what we (Western colonizers) did to other Indigenous peoples, we did first to ourselves. The arrival of Christianity throughout Europe occurred gradually and often violently, assimilating and obliterating the existing Indigenous traditions.

The Witchcraze, or Burning Times, started in the late 1300s and finally ended 500 years later in the early 1800s. In 1484, Pope Innocent VIII published a papal edict authorizing the use of torture to elicit confessions of Witchcraft (which has yet to be rescinded). Two years later, two German monks published a handbook called the *Malleus Maleficarum*, an anti-woman screed on how to fulfill the Pope's orders, and in 1542, Pope Paul III established the Holy Office of the Inquisition (which also continues to this day).

Mostly women, but also children and men, were accused of practicing Witchcraft, consorting with the Devil, causing the climate's sudden cooling and casting evil spells to harm livestock, crops and humans. They were imprisoned, tortured and murdered by religious and secular institutions. The terror spread across the Atlantic, where 25 women and men were executed as Witches in colonial North America, and the Spanish and Portuguese Inquisitions brought terror to Indigenous peoples throughout the Americas.

The Witchcraze has been called the women's holocaust. A mere accusation could lead to death, and during this prolonged terror women lost all rights to personal control or autonomy. They weren't allowed to learn to read, let alone receive an education. They couldn't inherit or own property and were themselves considered the property of their father, brother or husband. Their traditional roles as shamans and healers, midwives and wise women who were central to the spiritual and physical wellbeing of their villages either disappeared, went underground or shape-shifted into a more socially acceptable form, as it did for their male counterparts and their traditions.

Some academics have disputed that the Witchcraze was a persecution of practicing Witches, but other scholars, like Carlo Ginzburg, argue that the trial transcripts, along with other evidence, confirm the existence and suppression of Indigenous, shamanic traditions practiced by *benandanti* and *streghe*, *wicce*, *noaidi*, *gonagas*, *volur*, *seidkonur*, *tietaja* and others throughout Europe.

Shards of Europe's shamanic practices survived, morphing into folk traditions, herbal lore or even Church calendars and saintly figures, with bits of magic discreetly practiced today by the women who go to Church on Sunday or the men who dance on village greens on May Day.

But painful reverberations of this persecution continue for women, and men, for the Earth and Spirit, with lingering mischaracterizations of Wicca, and Witches, and ongoing constraints on women's freedom, power and spiritual roles, and with devastating impact on the Earth and our souls. Today, violence continues with the torture and murder of accused Witches in once-colonized Africa, India, Nepal and elsewhere.

Despite this brutal history, Wicca has reemerged, and there's an aura of magic about its return.

Rebirth

In the early 1930s, a remarkable group of English iconoclasts went looking for the religion of their ancestors. Why that moment? Perhaps it was a reaction to 100 years of the Industrial Revolution, with its damage to land and people, and the punishing effects of World War I and the Great Depression.

Inspiration may also have come from the counterculture of Romantics, Spiritualists, Suffragists, Theosophists and the esoteric, magical movement made famous by the Hermetic Order of the Golden Dawn – a metaphysical society founded in the late 19th and early 20th centuries with such prestigious members as Lady Gregory and the poet W.B. Yeats – all looking for a different kind of divinity that included the Feminine Principle. Or maybe it was Mother Earth calling her children home.

These intrepid souls lived in the midst of massive stone circles, colossal mounds and chalk giants carved into hillsides, stories of fairies and myths of Avalon, the Green Knight and Sir Gawain, seasonal stag-antlered dances and the faces of Green Men carved in churches, Goddesses named Bride, Brigid and Brigantia, from whom some say the name Britain came, and Gods of the forest such as Cernunnos and Herne. There was seasonal rejoicing remembered in local folk traditions and preserved within the Christian calendar, and old Gods and Goddesses thinly disguised as saints. Everything was amber in which proof of an earlier life resided.

There was also the revolutionary theory of a brilliant Egyptologist and Suffragist, Dr. Margaret Murray, the 'grandmother of Wicca.' Murray's book, *The Witch-Cult in Western Europe*, published by Oxford University Press in 1921, argued that Witchcraft had been a pan-European religion with beliefs, ritual and organization as highly developed as that of any. Though largely discredited years later, Murray had hit upon signs of something sacred in England, and Europe, before Christianity.

Whatever the inspiration, it's difficult to retrieve a religion from shattered shards and a bad reputation. However, three covens, or groups, appeared in England: in Hampshire's New Forest and in Norfolk and Cheshire. The covens were discreet and hidden, but in 1951, the Witchcraft Law of 1735 was repealed and Witchcraft burst into the public's awareness in the person of Gerald Gardner, a retired British civil servant who said he'd been initiated by the New Forest coven.

Gardner wrote several of the first books on Witchcraft by a practitioner and spoke publicly and to the press – no small feat given the lingering stereotypes. And he worked with some of the most important women in Wicca, like Doreen Valiente, the coven's High Priestess. Valiente wrote the famous Goddess invocation *The Charge of the Goddess*, and she and Gardner fleshed out the rites and practices that formed the foundation of the Gardnerian tradition.

Gardner claimed that he practiced the religion Murray had described, calling it Wicca, and her theory became Wicca's well-accepted 'myth of origin.' Years later, after careful scrutiny, historians and practitioners concluded that the Gardnerian tradition was not an unbroken, hereditary, pan-European tradition matching Murray's theory.

Gardner and Valiente had woven a creative and effective magic carpet from Murray's theory, surviving elements of Euro-Indigenous traditions – including Anglo-Saxon and Celtic influences, folk practices and lore – classical scholarship and Western Mystery, hermetic and esoteric schools, Freemasonry, even aspects of Eastern wisdom.

Today, many still subscribe to Murray's theory as literal truth, but other Wiccans appreciate her recognition of archetypal truths that continue to resonate – a Great Mother Goddess, a Horned God of forest and field, a small community organized into groups (covens) with trained Priestesses and Priests, the use of ecstatic practices, the celebration of seasonal holy days and lunar rites, initiation rites and the keeping of a book of wisdom called the Book of Shadows.

Whether there were surviving, hidden and hereditary traditions or an inspired new religious movement with ancient roots had been born, Gardner offered the world spiritual techniques and insights that people valued and needed – most notably feminine divinity, spiritual leadership for women, spiritual practices providing personal experiences of an immanent divinity, reverence for the Earth and attunement with Nature's wisdom. And real, divine magic.

Wicca took root and began to grow beyond the British Isles with the rediscovery of other forgotten

Euro-Indigenous traditions and pantheons of deities from faiths that existed before the Abrahamic religions (Judaism, Christianity and Islam), especially Goddesses, which were integrated into Wiccan practice and cosmology. Women found a spiritual home that honored them as spiritual leaders; publishing and the internet connected people and provided support, community and access to once hidden information; leaders who were unafraid of persecution emerged into the public eye to challenge stereotypes; and the movement grew and spawned a broader revival of Euro-Indigenous and modern 'Pagan' traditions.

Today, there are many variations and diverse lineages and traditions in Wicca, each with its own organizational structure. Many have incorporated as religious organizations, churches or temples and, while the law and academics now recognize Wicca as a religion, many practitioners prefer the term spirituality. In formal surveys, the number of adherents of Wicca varies from a few hundred thousand to several million globally. Wiccans are lawyers, doctors, rock stars, truck drivers, dog trainers and Unitarian ministers and as likely to be your neighbor next door as your dentist. Wiccans are, literally, everywhere.

Wicca's legitimacy does not need to be derived from its past but from the profound, transformative spiritual experiences, insights and values it offers practitioners every day. In this sense, Wicca is a new religious movement, and its (re)birth is one of the most rare and significant events in human history.

What do so many people believe?

Wicca is not a belief system

One of the first things I loved about Wicca was that I wasn't asked to believe anything. I wasn't asked to accept anyone else's word for who God is, or isn't, or what God wants me to do or not do, or even if there *is* a God. I wasn't asked to believe in a Goddess either. Honestly, I'd have run out the door if anyone had said '*Just believe*.'

The Priestesses simply started practicing. They didn't explain what they were doing or why they were doing it. It was unfamiliar, and frankly, it made me uncomfortable. But the part of me that responded to beauty and poetry, music and movement, that was curious and open to joy, that was a feminist, that trusted my instincts and my heart, the part of me that had been called, all those unschooled and wise parts of me experienced something I'd never felt before: the extraordinary and divine energy generated when women (and men) come together in a circle and honor the Divine as not just male but *female*. I kept going back and the feeling kept growing.

I felt it as I cast circles alone in my tiny studio apartment in Manhattan, danced beneath a full Moon, or meditated in the new ways I'd learned in circle. I felt my own energies – my mental focus, my emotions, even my body – shifting with the changing Moon and cycling seasons. When my menstrual cycle moved into rhythm with the Moon *and* the other women in my circle, I experienced my periods not as a messy or uncomfortable inconvenience but as part of my life-giving power, and I noticed what I'd always ignored – a heightened psychic sensitivity that I learned to honor and cultivate.

I began to understand the meaning of the words and gestures, the names and gifts of the Goddesses and Gods from all over the world, the wisdom waiting within the natural world around and within me. I could *feel* the life, joy and love flowing all around and through me. I felt my spirit coming alive and I recognized the Spirit living in the world around me. It felt like magic. And it felt utterly natural. Turns out, Wiccans don't believe in God or Goddess any more than you believe in air or a tree or the dog, or cat, lying beside you.

Wicca is a spiritual practice

Wicca is a wisdom tradition and a system of spiritual practices that *anyone* can master, regardless of their age, gender, race, culture or even religion. Wicca is a path of personal enlightenment, empowerment and responsibility. Your experiences with the Sacred, your visions and insights, will be as unique as you are.

But it's not a subjective reality. As you work, especially with others, you'll find you're having similar experiences, encounters and insights. And your visions and experiences will be confirmed by the living universe. Your confidence will grow. Most wonderful of all, even at its most extraordinary and magical, practicing Wicca feels like you're remembering something you already knew, awakening a divine gift that's utterly natural, coming home to a divinity that was there all along.

Finding yourself in the presence of the Sacred changes everything; finding the Sacred present within yourself changes *you*. Some changes happen in an instant, as if you really did wave a magic wand or chant magic words. But other changes take time and patience – you can't make the grass grow by tugging on it.

Change takes self-awareness, courage and effort. You have to change cultural and childhood conditioning that gets in the way of your dreams, your gifts, your purpose – and that may include lingering stereotypes about Witches. That's a lot of work. But Wicca gives you the tools, wisdom and magic to do that work.

Realizing you're living in a sacred world also means you have to be very brave and really look at what's wrong in the world around us: why it's wounded and out of balance. You have to take responsibility to help fix what human beings have broken, to heal what we've wounded. That's *really* a lot of work. And it can be very difficult because most of the world's cultures are blind and indifferent to the divinity embodied by Creation.

The social and environmental crises we've created are all symptoms of our mistaken belief that the Divine either doesn't exist or exists 'out there,' somewhere else, and that Spirit is transcendent 'light' beyond the world and the bodies in which we live. But everything we need is within and all around us. The Sacred is within and all around us. The practices unleash that life-transforming, sustaining and empowering connection, and there are spirits and guides all along the way to help us.

To practice Wicca is to become a wise one – the one who sees and moves between the worlds knowing that the worlds are one, that the realm of Spirit is the soul of the world and the world embodies that Spirit. That is the key to unlocking the real, divine magic of life. The invisible will become visible, and the visible numinous.

Chapter 2

Divinity

One lonely afternoon when I was about six years old, with half my friends disappearing to Hebrew schools and the other half in Catholic schools, I asked my mother what religion were we and who God was.

She looked startled, then smiled and sat me down. 'People think they need God to tell them the difference between right and wrong, to punish them when they're bad and reward them when they're good.' My mother spoke slowly, carefully.

'Your father and I don't believe that. We believe in the goodness of the human heart, and that we're each responsible for the world we live in, for making it a good world to live in. All you really need is the Golden Rule: Do unto others as you would have them do unto you.'

She paused, watching me as the thought sank in. 'Does that make sense to you?' she asked.

'Yes,' I nodded. 'Treat people the way you want them to treat you.' I thought about Joan, my friend across the street, in her white Communion dress.

'But who is God?' I asked. 'Is he real?'

'That's a big question that adults have been fighting about for centuries,' my mother replied. 'If it still interests you when you're grown up, you can look for an answer then.'

As I said earlier, I was satisfied with those answers, until something very different than the God of my childhood friends came looking for me. The divinity that calls to *you*, the form that It, She, He, They take on a hilltop in Ireland, a cave in Crete, or in a book read on a rattling subway train, whoever it is, whatever and wherever that expression appears, the revelation is *yours* and will be respected by other Wiccans.

The diversity of Wiccan divinity

Most faiths have specific theologies and views of deity, like the Abrahamic faiths most of us have grown up with that personify divinity as a Father God, sometimes with a Son, or as transcendent and non-gendered, though always described with male vocabulary.

Modern Wicca accepts that you can have an entirely different view of divinity than someone else who also considers themselves Wiccan, and Wiccan perspectives are diverse. There are Wiccans who honor divinity as both female and male, or duotheistic (like the Taoist yin and yang), which was revolutionary in Western culture (the Hebrew Shekinah was largely hidden, Mary was not divine, and any Muslim feminine expression is heavily veiled). For some Wiccans, especially Gardnerians, divinity is revered as the Great Mother Goddess and the Horned God of animals and the wild things.

There are Wiccans who recognize divinity as Mother Earth and the Triple Goddess of Maiden, Mother and Crone reflected in the Moon (and in women), and God as Son and Lover of the Goddess, as Green Man, God of Vegetation and Kings of Oak and Holly, and as the Sun God.

For many Wiccans, the Goddess and God are the Divine Couple who embody love as the energy of the cosmos. They are lovers, Mother and Son, Crone and Youth, Maiden and Lord of Time/Death; whatever forms they take, the Goddess and God are always connected in a life-generating relationship. Between the two poles they embody lies the full range of Creation's diversity unified by the bonds of love. Together, they are One, beyond gender or polarity.

Some Wiccans consider themselves polytheists honoring many different Goddesses and Gods who are distinct beings, often associated with particular places or pantheons of non-Abrahamic cultures across the globe.

For other Wiccans, the many Goddesses are aspects of one Great Goddess and the many Gods aspects of one Great God. And some Wiccans, like the Dianic tradition, are monotheistic, honoring only the Goddess as the singular Source of Creation, or divinity that's neither feminine nor masculine.

There are Wiccans for whom deities are entities with a literal existence and other Wiccans who view deities as Jungian archetypes or as symbols of underlying forces of Creation. And many Wiccans share a pantheistic perspective, viewing Goddesses and Gods as personifications of the life force manifested in Creation, as embodiments of the forces of Nature and anthropomorphic manifestations of a particular type of energy or power.

And many Wiccans combine many of these views or prefer to use non-gendered language like Beloved and Lover, still recognizing the creative polarity of Creation but leaving behind heteronormative language and limitations. Wiccans also encounter and work with the spirit beings of Nature like spirits of place, elementals (spirits of the elements), fairies and more, described by some as an animistic worldview.

When I'm asked which view I take, my reply is always 'Yes.'

Clear your view

We'll explore some of these views in upcoming chapters and also what's most often shared by all Wiccans – the rediscovery of ancient and ancestral deities that pre-date Christianity, encounters within the realms of Spirit, experiences of divinity embodied and present in the natural world and therefore accessible and willing, when properly approached, to engage with humanity, and divinity as a Mystery just beyond the reach of understanding, pulling us forward into an endless dance of discovery.

Talking *about* divinity can never take the place of experiences *with* divinity. So, let's take off the blindfolds tied on by a world that has taught us God is male, beyond reach or comprehension, or that nothing is sacred. Let's see the Mystery hiding in plain sight.

Purification is a simple, powerful technique that gets the blindfold off. You don't purify because you're born with original sin, or because, if you're a woman who menstruates, you're impure, or you've eaten a forbidden food or touched someone who is taboo. For Wiccans, the human spirit and body, Nature's spirit and body, are sacred. But we live in a human world that's messy and stressful, full of worries, doubts and distortions.

If I think I'm not good enough, I'm blocked from fulfilling my dreams and my potential. If I think I'm not worthy of love, an obstacle stands between my heart and my happiness. If I think God is judging me, or is elsewhere and indifferent, or the world I live in is inanimate and indifferent, my ideas separate me from the Sacred.

Purification helps us clean out wounds so they can heal, removes obstacles and unblocks the natural movement of energy to and through us, with life-sustaining power. It clarifies our thinking, our hearts and our spirits, freeing us to see clearly, feel fully and be present with our souls, the Sacred and the world.

There are all sorts of ways to purify, many using Nature's elements like Air, Water or Fire. Here's a familiar, simple and effective purification using water and salt (to represent the element Earth).

Practice: Salt water purification

At home

Sprinkle salt into a bowl of warm water. You can also do this in a bathtub or shower.

❖ Wash your hands. Take your time. If you wish, you can say: *'I cleanse my hands so all my actions are undertaken with good intent.'*

❖ Touch the salt water to your forehead/third eye and say: *'I cleanse my eyes and my thoughts to see and think clearly.'*

❖ Touch the salt water to your heart and say: *'I cleanse my heart to feel the love, compassion and joy that reside there.'*

❖ Touch the salt water to your stomach and say: *'I cleanse the fire in my belly, so all my power is available to me for good purpose and a good life.'*

❖ Touch the salt water to your feet and say: *'I cleanse my feet, so I walk gently and with gratitude upon Mother Earth.'*

❖ Take your time and allow yourself to feel the release of energies at each point of purification. Release what you need to. Let it go. Cry if you're moved to – tears are salt water, the body's way of purifying.

❖ Wash your face. Pour the bowl over your hands, and watch as the water disappears down the drain, taking your sorrows and worries, obstacles and inhibitions, bad habits and patterns away with it.

Thank the salt water returning to the sea for lending you its cleansing gifts. Enjoy the feelings of clarity, freedom and release.

In the sea

As soon as you can, bathe in the sea. Feel the water wake you, the tidal push and pull against your body, the blood in your veins coursing to the same rhythm. Taste the salt on your lips.

❖ Float, arms stretched out, Sun on your face, using whatever you need to stay buoyant. Feel yourself weightless and free. Feel yourself cradled body, heart and soul.

❖ Let the salt water draw off the toxins of sorrow, the bitterness of what remains unfulfilled, the obstructions that you're ready to release. Float and let go. Release whatever you need to. Let yourself be cleansed.

❖ When you're ready, return to the land. Feel yourself cleansed, renewed, reborn from the waters of love.

Experiencing divinity

Purification helps free you from the false ideas and feelings separating you from your own inner divinity and from the divinity of the natural world that you're a part of. It enables you to be fully present to the presence of divinity. 'Yes, but how do I *experience* the Divine?' I can hear you asking. You already have.

Guided meditation: Divine presence

You can recite and record this guided meditation, and then listen to it as you practice, or read it first and then imagine. Find a spot, inside or out, where you can sit undisturbed. Turn off your phone, sit comfortably and close your eyes.

Let's begin.

You're going to remember what you already know.

Breathe deeply, inhaling and exhaling completely. Five full breaths. Relax your body, tensing and releasing your muscles from the top of your head to the bottom of your toes, continuing to breathe fully and deeply.

When you're ready, focus on the memory of an occasion when you were aware of the presence of the Divine. Bring it fully and clearly to your mind's eye. What did you see? See it clearly. What were you doing when it happened? Where were you? See your surroundings clearly. When did it happen? How old were you? See yourself clearly.

Remember what happened. Bring the events, the images and the sensation clearly to mind. How did you feel? Focus on the physical feelings you experienced. Did you feel a tingling sensation rush through your body? Did you get goose bumps? Did you feel a rush of heat? Did you feel your heart race? Feel them again.

Focus on the emotions you experienced. Did you feel startled, exhilarated, peaceful? Did your feelings change? Did you feel awe, joy, love? Feel them again. What happened? Did you begin to cry? To laugh, sing, pray? Take your time. Remember the sense of presence you experienced. Feel it again. Ask the Divine, Goddess, God, or both, to be with you and to guide you. Stay in your physical/emotional feelings.

When you're ready, say thank you. Open your eyes. Rest in the feelings. Write about your experiences in your magical journal.

Paying attention

You have an innate ability to experience the Sacred. Feeling that connection is the source of magic that creates a life of fulfillment, harmony and love.

Paying attention to the physical feelings of your first encounter with the Sacred is a reliable way to recognize *and* to invite the presence of the Sacred. It's an age-old shamanic method with practical usefulness as well: practitioners of Wicca (and Reiki) rely on the physical sensations of light, heat and divine energies when sending and receiving healing energies.

From the very beginning, when the Goddess first called to me and ever since, I experience a rush of energy followed by goose bumps, a perception of everything brightening and then a sense of presence, as if the air is charged with electricity. That's followed by joy, peace and love. However you experience it physically, what you're feeling emotionally is *wonder*, even ecstasy. It's what we feel when we experience something marvelous, miraculous, magical. It's what we feel when we experience the Sacred. So, pay attention to your physical and emotional feelings.

You'll also learn to pay attention to and cultivate other signs and senses, like premonitions and synchronicities, dreams and visions, encounters in altered states and more, which we'll explore. Your encounters will grow in number and frequency as you increasingly let go of the old stories of separation from the Sacred and the false consciousness that has created (that God is off in Heaven, that the natural, material world, like our bodies, is 'less' than Spirit and ours to exploit, and that human beings have 'fallen from grace') and shift your awareness to the sense of presence that comes when you pay attention.

And that's my definition of a Witch:
A person who's paying attention
to the presence of the Divine.

But how do we learn to pay attention in the midst of all the stress and distractions of daily life? It's actually simple. Create a daily or regular practice that evokes the physical sensations you have in the presence of divinity. You'll know it's working when you experience wonder.

Practice: Paying attention to divinity

When you wake up, before your day begins, take a moment to focus on being back in your body. Stretch, open the blinds and greet the world.

❖ Greet the Sun. Be present. Be grateful.

❖ Feel the warmth on your face and feel the life-giving energy fill you. Inhale.

❖ Feel the energy moving through you, vitalizing you for the rest of the day. See the world illuminated.

❖ Look for one vivid expression of natural beauty. Even in a city you'll find it – the blue sky, a cloud, a bird.

❖ Give thanks for another day of life and start your day.

My morning ritual includes greeting my beloved, the Sun, water, joyful dog, feeding the birds, Honoring the Four Directions, which we'll explore later. It begins my day in the right way – with love, connection, vitality, and gratitude. Practice paying attention to divinity every day and you'll change the way you experience the world.

**Creation embodies the Sacred. Divinity is
everywhere present in the natural world.
Everything that exists – you and other people,
plants and animals, Earth and sky, air and
water, seasons and weather, Moon and Sun,
stars and galaxies, quarks and quanta, matter**

**and anti-matter, the seen and unseen, the
manifest and the mysterious – is a form, an
embodiment, an expression of divinity.**

That is what you see when the blindfold comes off –
the Mystery hiding in plain sight. Once you experience
that reality, everything changes. *You* change. And that
unlocks the magic at the heart of Wicca.

A breath away

Breathing can become one of your most powerful
practices for experiencing divinity. It's the first thing you
did when you arrived here and it's the last thing you'll do
when you leave. We do it constantly, without thinking,
unaware that with every breath we take, the Divine is just
a breath away.

Conscious breathing, or breath meditation, is one of the
first things we do when we cast circle, and it's a skill you
can use anywhere, any time. It's also the foundation for
powerful magical techniques and much more that we'll
explore later. Let's begin with the essentials of how
breathing and breath meditation work.

First, breathing is a natural way to purify. Your body is
cleansed each time you exhale carbon dioxide. Breathing
meditation cleans away your mental clutter and your
physical tensions. When your mind is clear, you perceive
clearly. After all, it's impossible to hear the voice of
the Sacred if your mind is chaotically chattering, and

impossible to receive wisdom and energy if your body is tense and blocked. With each breath, your body and mind become relaxed, still and quiet. Gradually, your awareness shifts and you are fully present in the moment.

Beginners often worry that they won't be able to keep their mind from wandering and getting cluttered again, even for a few minutes, let alone longer. I have good news: your mind *will* naturally wander, even if you've been practicing for many years, and that's ok.

There's a trick to meditation: understand and accept that thoughts will enter your mind. Let them come and let them go. Just notice and release. And don't give yourself a hard time. There's another trick: when your mind wanders, simply bring your attention back to your breath. That will bring you back to the present moment. Breathing gives you something to return to when your mind drifts away to a thought, a memory of the past or worry about the future. Use your breathing to focus. This is also the purpose of using a mantra, a word or symbol, which we'll explore soon. And remember: don't criticize yourself.

Learning that it's natural for my mind to wander, and that I could use my breathing to return to being present, made all the difference for me. No more performance anxiety. I was able to sit for 5 minutes, then 10, and finally as long as I wanted or needed. My mind still wanders, but I no longer get hung up with self-criticism. Instead, I notice my mind is wandering, I let go of the thought and return my focus to my breathing. I'm once again present in the moment. Among other benefits, it's helped me become gentle with myself and to accept myself. And that has been incredibly useful in so many other areas of my perfectionist life.

Everyone's meditating these days. The practical benefits of the practice are widely known – from better health to improved concentration and even greater success in business. There's another important reason to integrate breathing meditation into our spiritual toolbox: *divinity is just a breath away*.

Guided meditation: Breathing

You can recite and record the following text and then listen to it as you practice, or read it first and then imagine. You can do this guided meditation anywhere; outside is always best. Find a spot that calls to you, and where you can sit undisturbed. If you're inside, sit or lie comfortably. Hang a 'do not disturb' sign on your bedroom door and close it. And don't forget to turn off your phone.

Let's begin.

Close your eyes. Breathe deeply – exhaling completely and inhaling slowly and fully. Feel your body grow relaxed, your mind quiet. Inhale slowly and fully and feel the oxygen entering you, filling your lungs, carried by your blood, pumped by your heart. Feel the oxygen moving through every cell of your body. Feel it energizing you with life.

Exhale and feel the carbon dioxide leaving you. As it leaves, relax your body, starting at the top of your head. With each breath that you exhale, feel the relaxation moving downward, through your neck and shoulders, arms and fingers, chest and pelvis, thighs and calves and feet and toes. Exhale and relax. Inhale slowly and fully, holding the breath for a count of three, mind growing quiet and still. Exhale completely, body growing quiet and still.

Continue breathing, allowing your mind to become clear; allowing thoughts to move through, like a leaf carried on the wind, just noticing as they arise and letting them float away. Return your focus to your breathing – slow and steady, in and out. Mind growing still and body relaxing.

Continue for five full breaths, in and out. Breathe in and hold the breath for a count of three. Feel the energy coursing through you, nourishing you, sustaining you, energizing you. Exhale completely. Continue breathing deeply and fully. Feel your connection to the divine energy of Creation. Feel the energy of Creation coursing through you, nourishing you, blessing you.

When you're ready, open your eyes.

You are never alone. Every breath connects you to the Sacred.

Chapter 3

Magic

We live in a culture that dismisses magic as silly superstition. We believe in scientific, rational explanations, but yesterday's magic is today's science. Where science leaves off, magic begins again. It dwells at the limits of what we understand. And just as you can experience divinity, you can experience magic.

The extraordinary, mysterious and wonderful that awakens within and that manifests in the world without warning, explanation or apparent cause happens to all of us. And when it does, we say with amazement, 'It was magical!'

Deep inside, we long for the magic to make our dreams come true. It may be why you're reading this book, impatiently waiting for spells and incantations, for the real secrets to change your life. Wicca has always been a magical spirituality. But be careful what you ask for... because magic works.

We live in an age of instant gratification, and that's how a lot of people think about magic – they want the spell, the incantation and the potion that works. Simple and easy. Since Wicca came out of the broom closet, there have been countless books, endless websites, YouTube videos and online classes offering 'secret' spells and 'ancient' incantations, powerful potions and all that you could possibly want or need for instant, magical gratification.

Sometimes it even works. More often it doesn't, and then people throw out the concoctions and conclude that magic isn't real. They shut the book, blow out the candle and ring the bell. I don't want that to be *you*, because I know magic is real. I know that your life, like the world, can be filled with magic. I want that for you. I want that for the world.

Magic misunderstood

To understand what real, divine magic is, you first have to understand what it *isn't*. People have been approaching magic with some very strange ideas that have nothing to do with real magic.

❖ Magic is not awakened with an incantation, formula or spell.

❖ Magic is not about bending the world to your will.

❖ Magic is not about controlling secret forces of Nature.

❖ Magic doesn't happen by learning to command the supernatural.

❖ Magic is not manipulative, mechanical or Machiavellian.

❖ Magic is not about managing the cosmos as if it were a machine.

Those are all ideas left over from patriarchal views of reality – the old one in which God gave man dominion over an inanimate world to do with as he pleases, or the modern one in which man has the intellectual power to unlock the laws of a mechanical and inanimate universe to then manipulate and exploit for his own ends.

That kind of 'magic' is about ego and domination. The universe is *not* a machine to be maneuvered, whether by science or magic. You can have all the props and potions and plans, and enough ego, intention and willpower to run for president, but unless you understand the secrets of magic, casting spells will be like driving a car without gas. You may get a mile or two down the road but ultimately you're not going anywhere. Thank goodness. Imagine the world if it were that simple and easy.

But real magic, *divine* magic, is simple and easy. It's utterly natural.

The secret of real magic

Magic isn't something you do *to* the world. Magic is what a living cosmos does *with* you once you've awakened to its divinity, and yours. The secret to *real* magic is your partnership with divinity – because the energy that makes all magic work is divine. Just as all of Creation is an embodiment of the Divine, all real magic is a manifestation of the Divine.

When you're open, aware and connected, magic is everywhere: in the synchronicities, signs and messages you receive; in the dreams that come true; in the healing that defies prognosis; in the opportunities that appear and the unexpected help, healing and harmony with which your life begins to take shape; in the destiny that begins to manifest and the love that arrives when you've given up. And much more.

When I wrote my first memoir, *Book of Shadows*, I realized magic wasn't just the spells we cast that so often worked. The greatest magic was the extraordinary way the Divine began to appear in my daily life. *Magic changes everything and the first thing it changes is you.* It rattles your cage and breaks down your barriers; it shifts your perception and awakens your soul. It's as if you've been living in a black-and-white movie that's suddenly filled with color. Magic is a dimension of reality now open to you, a dimension of yourself now known to you.

Magic is the vital, numinous quality of Creation.

The magic that you *make* by spellcasting, ritual, meditating, dancing, chanting, lovemaking, art creating, poem writing, vision seeking, self-care, being in Nature, visiting the Other World, giving thanks, or however you choose, works because the power you're working with is divine. And the more you work with it, the more you'll realize it's the *power of love*. Magic manifests in your life because of your connection to the Sacred. Like the sacred isle of Avalon, magic will also disappear in the mists, but once you know it's there, you can always find it again.

Changing consciousness at will

Just as there are ways of inviting the Sacred into your life – which we'll continue to explore and develop in upcoming chapters – there are ways to invite magic into your life and to begin to magically co-create a divinely empowered life. Dion Fortune, author and member of the Hermetic Order of the Golden Dawn, defined magic as 'the art of changing consciousness at will.' It's an important definition but not the only way to experience or make magic.

Shamans, Wiccans, Witches and mystics of many faiths have long known that altering our state of consciousness opens us to the Divine; it enables us to enter the realms of Spirit, to move freely outside the bounds of space and time and to dive deep within.

You've already begun to make the magic of changing consciousness at will – with meditation. It's one of the fastest, easiest and most powerful ways to change your consciousness, and it will temporarily alter your brain the very first time you try it. Neuroscience is verifying that, practiced consistently over time, meditation alters your brain permanently, expanding its volume, areas of activation and brain wave production.

Meditation, like magic, changes you. Studies are confirming that meditation reduces anxiety and depression and increases creativity, imagination, visualization skills and memory, attentiveness and calmness within the mind *and* body. It improves perception, learning ability, concentration, self-awareness and self-control.

And when the meditation practice focuses loving attention on the heart region, the meditator develops the capacity to feel love and compassion toward themselves, and then others. Long-term practice leads to permanent changes in the brain and an expanded capacity to focus and learn, and to feel happiness, compassion and loving-kindness toward others when we're *not* meditating. People describe it as bliss.

Wiccan meditation has yet to be studied; however, practitioners describe similar effects, which makes sense since we commonly use very similar techniques. Meditation also connects us to the Sacred, and as our relationship deepens, we become one with the real power that makes magic manifest.

Another secret

Shamans, Wiccans, Witches and mystics have always known what science is beginning to discover – that the mind has profound capacities to affect the outcome of events. (Another area of forgotten human capacities that neurobiology and quantum physics are beginning to explore and affirm.) Changing consciousness unlocks forgotten human abilities that are... magical. Meditation is a universal, natural and effective way to change consciousness – it's also an ancient and powerful technique for making magic.

People generally think that a *mantra*, which means 'sound tool' in Sanskrit, is used to keep our mind from wandering off during meditation. Like breath, it gives us something to focus on. But there's magic in the method waiting to be unleashed:

What you focus on during your meditation, while you're in an altered state of consciousness and connected to the Divine – the mantra, phrase, word, symbol, image or intention – manifests.

Affirmations – repetition of positive phrases to alter our self-perception and behavior and to manifest desired changes in our psyche and our life – are a modern adaptation. Louise Hay understood and helped others understand the power of affirmations to change one's consciousness and one's life. You'll find similar ideas about the power of intention in the Law of Attraction, Deepak Chopra's Vedantic teachings, *A Course in Miracles*, the New Thought Movement, the visualization work of Shakti Gawain, and scores of others, including the spells of Wiccans.

Reframe an affirmation in the context of your connection to the Sacred, use it while in an altered, opened state of awareness, and it's like putting rocket fuel in your engine. It's an enchantment.

Enchantment

I'm a bit of a detective, which is why I like etymology, the study of the origin and development of language. There is lost wisdom, and magic, hidden in the meaning of words, and this is one of my favorites: the root of *enchant* is the Latin *incantare*, which meant to enchant or fix a spell *by singing*.

Chanting is one of the most joyful ways to alter our consciousness (which has been scientifically proven) *and* make magic. A magical chant can be an imitation of a sound of Nature, a single letter with profound symbolic meaning, a word or a phrase that expresses your intention or goal. It can also be the name of a deity. If you can make your chant rhyme – a common characteristic of many spells, as you'll learn later – and give it a tempo, even better. It turns out that the brain responds positively to rhymes, rhythms and repetition.

Chanting with others magnifies the effect. I learned to chant when I began practicing yoga many years ago, but it was even more powerful when I chanted in my Wiccan circles. Studies have shown that group chanting actually synchronizes the brain waves and energies between the members of a circle. When we chant together, we're aligning our minds, bodies and spirits with one another. We're literally coming into harmony – each voice unique but together creating something magically magnified. Alone or with others, we're aligning with Creation, especially when we use chants that emulate the sounds of Creation. That's making magic.

Now that you know some of the secrets, you can make magic by chanting a vivid and empowering phrase as you meditate, alter your consciousness, connect to the Sacred Source, focus on your intention, and begin to manifest your reason for being here.

Practice: Magical chanting

Give some thought to a word or short phrase(s) that expresses what you want to change, accomplish or create in your life. Don't overthink. Let your playful side have some fun composing a rhyme that you enjoy.

❖ You can use this adaptation of a wise Louise Hay affirmation:
'I am one with the divine power that created me. I use my power with love, success and generosity.'

❖ I also recommend this classic and powerful Wiccan chant to get your creative and magical energies moving for positive change:
'She changes everything She touches and everything She touches, changes.'

❖ Recite your chant a few times, and when you've got it, write it in your magical journal and memorize it.

Sit comfortably in a place where you won't be disturbed. Close your eyes. Breathe until you feel your mind and body grow quiet and peaceful. Feel the energy coursing through you and all around you.

Feel your consciousness shift and your perception become clearer. Feel your heart open. Feel yourself increasingly connected to the Sacred. You're coming into union and wholeness. Thank Creation for receiving your intention, your energy, your magic.

Inhale fully and naturally. Chant your enchantment as you exhale. Inhale deeply and rest in silence, feeling the power and potential of Creation flow through you. Chant your enchantment as you exhale. Chant with joy. Allow yourself to rest in the silence as you continue inhaling and exhaling naturally.

Now chant as you inhale and exhale, from your diaphragm. Feel the vibration travel through you. Enjoy the feelings the vibration creates within and beyond your body. Feel the source of Creation that is within you. Feel your intention moving out into the world, with joy.

Chant until you feel fulfilled. When you're done, rest in the silence and the sense of happiness, peace and bliss. Thank Creation for accepting your energy, your intention, your magic into itself and for returning it to you in the form you've envisioned, or the unexpected form that's best for your wellbeing and happiness. When you're ready, open your eyes. Rest in the feelings evoked in you – the changes you feel in your heart, your mind, your spirit.

Congratulations – you just created your first spell. Write it in your magical journal.

Pay attention to shifts in your feelings and your energy. Watch for signs of manifestation in your life and in the world around you. It may be subtle at first, but if you take a few minutes a few times a week to make magic with your focused meditation and nourish the enchantment, like a seed planted in spring, your intention will take root and grow.

Practice magical chanting regularly and you'll start to recognize that consciousness is much more than thinking. And so is magic. You're entering the generative flow of Creation. And that's where real magic comes from.

> **What you chant, repeat, visualize, imagine evokes change within you and in the world.**

Visualization

Just as sound can alter your consciousness and a phrase can help your magic manifest, an image or symbol can provide a visual focus for meditation and for magic. In traditional magical parlance, what you focus on and project energy into (which we'll discuss soon) is called a 'thought form.' It's also called 'setting your intention,' a phrase that you may be familiar with.

You can't manifest your magic, your goal, intention or desire if you can't visualize it first. Visualization practices help you focus on your intention with precision, clarity and confidence. You'll discover it gets easier when you practice for a few minutes regularly – one or two minutes a day should be enough – rather than for longer stretches infrequently. Visualization skills also provide a powerful foundation for other important practices – including entering visionary or trance states – that we'll explore shortly.

You're also going to work with other sensations that should make the technique easier to master, more fun and more useful. The more you *feel* what you're imagining, the more fully you can bring it into being. So let's practice visualizing, or creating a thought form.

Practice: Visualization 1

Begin with the Breathing guided meditation (*see page 32*).

1. When you feel relaxed and your mind is quiet, imagine a circle. See it clearly in your mind's eye.

2. Next, visualize the shape of a triangle, then a square. In your mind's eye, see them floating in space before you. If your mind wanders, simply bring it back to the shape you were visualizing. Work at a comfortable pace, practicing each step over as many sessions as you need.

3. When you're able to hold an image without distraction, spin it in space. Turn the two-dimensional circle into a sphere, the triangle into a pyramid, the square into a cube.

4. Next, visualize the sphere in different colors – moving through the spectrum from red to orange, yellow, green, blue, indigo, purple and then red again. Practice with the pyramid and the cube.

5. Visualize a variety of organic forms, such as an apple, a tree or your animal companion. It's helpful to look at them first, then close your eyes, breathe and visualize.

The next technique is particularly helpful if you have trouble visualizing. You're going to add more sensations to your practice.

Practice: Visualization 2

Just as you looked at the apple, or other organic form, before closing your eyes to visualize it, start with a physical experience and then re-create it with your imagination:

1. Light a white candle and look at it for several seconds. Now close your eyes and see the white candle: the flames dancing, the brightness of the light, the color and shape and movement. Repeat this practice until you can see the candle flame clearly and hold the image in your mind's eye.

2. Next, work on imagining heat by placing your hands near the candle so that you can feel its warmth against your skin, being careful not to burn yourself. Move your hands away, close your eyes and imagine the feeling of heat on your skin.

3. The next time you practice your visualization skills, don't light the candle – just visualize it and experience the feeling of warmth.

Retrieve your memories as clearly as you can and concentrate on them.

4. Work with other sensations. Imagine the way an orange feels, tastes and smells. Peel the orange, inhale its fragrance and taste the fruit. Then close your eyes and remember/imagine the sensations and, on another day, imagine seeing, peeling, smelling and tasting an orange without holding the real orange first.

Quantum magic, holy magic

Indigenous peoples who lived without industrial technologies developed technologies of the Sacred: our innate human spiritual capacities to participate with gratitude and grace, generosity and reverence in the tapestry of Creation. It is real magic.

We don't need science to explain spirituality. But as much as science *can* explain it, I like understanding why what we do actually works. Magic is natural after all, and the more we understand it, the more confidence we have in the reality of what we're experiencing. Quantum physics, neuroscience and other areas of study are confirming what shamans, Wiccans, Witches and mystics have long known. Everything is interconnected in countless ways that defy our old models of space, time, separation and causality. And our consciousness – which includes not only our mind but also our heart, body and spirit – can interact with this web of life, the energy of Creation.

Magic has always been used for practical purposes, like healing, assuring the abundance of a good harvest or hunt and experiencing the joys of love, and we'll explore the artistry of using magic for these and other purposes later.

A new definition of magic

Real magic is more than just changing consciousness at will or projecting will into thought forms to manifest our desires. We change consciousness to take off the blindfold and experience the Sacred that's everywhere present in Creation, including ourselves. Divine magic, *real* magic, flows not from ego and impulses but from our connection to the Sacred.

Magic is the life-altering awakening to the divinity within you and in the world around you. Magic is what manifests when you awaken. It's the next step in human evolution.

This is *my* definition and it is Wicca's great contribution to a world that's lost all sense of the Sacred. While the full measure of the Divine will always remain mysterious and ultimately unknowable (for no reason other than our human limitations), the world *embodies* divinity and so do you. And that's the source of real, divine magic.

Just as all of Creation is a manifestation of the Divine, all real magic is a manifestation of the Divine.

When you're connected with the Sacred Source of Creation, the Divine that dwells within you and the world around you, you'll discover that magic is a gift, a skill, a sacred practice to manifest the very best of who you are and what you want for your life. It's an extraordinary way to co-create your life with the Sacred.

The divine nature of the energy you'll work with transforms what you desire and how you make magic. Make magic with respect and reverence, joy and gratitude, humor and spontaneity. The more you nourish your relationship with divinity – within you and in the world around you – the easier and simpler and more natural magic becomes. It becomes a sixth sense, a quality of being, a revealed dimension that makes life an amazing and heroic adventure.

This book is my spell for you: *May you awaken to the divine magic of your life!*

Chapter 4

Spirit

For thousands of years, our ancestors knew about the Other World. Realms of Fairy and Seelie Court, Avalon the Isle of Apples, the Grail Castle and Chapel Perilus and Orbis Alius are names we remember, and great tales we still tell. These realms of Spirit, and the beings who inhabited them, would periodically appear to heroes and adventurers, to the seers and the wise ones who ventured forth in pursuit of wisdom and healings, blessings and even love.

For hundreds of years, other than the stories, the place names and a few sacred spots here on Earth where it was said you could gain entry, the Other World has remained hidden and invisible. But under the right conditions, with the right skills and the right magic, a door between the worlds will open. I know this because I have spent much of my life traveling there.

You're already developing skills that will help you – meditation, chanting and visualization all alter your consciousness and expand your perception. They remove the blindfold, enabling you to see the unseen and enter the Other World.

Once upon a time...

There are many shamanic techniques, called ecstatic practices, that enable you to gain access to the Other World; among them are dancing, drumming and journeying, fasting, ritual and working with sacred plants. There's also the age-old magic of storytelling, now called guided visualization. The right stories told in the right way for the right reasons can take you into the realms of Spirit.

Guided visualization: Storytelling

You can recite and record the following text and then listen to it. Have your magical journal nearby so you can write about your visions and experiences. Find a comfortable spot where you won't be disturbed; if you can work outside in Nature, even better.

Let's begin.

❖ Sit or lie down comfortably. Close your eyes. Breathe deeply and relax. Feel your body relaxing as you exhale, your mind becoming peaceful as you inhale. Place your hands over your heart and feel it steadily, rhythmically beating beneath them.

❖ Continue breathing slowly, deeply, fully inhaling and exhaling. Feel your breath moving outward into a widening space. Feel the breath that enters you moving deeper within you. Breathe in and out, connecting inner and outer, outer and beyond, beyond and within.

❖ Feel your consciousness changing, shifting, opening into the radiant dimensions within and beyond your physical body. As you continue to breathe, connected always to your heart, feel yourself rising, free to move anywhere.

In front of you is a door. This door only appears when you're ready to enter the realms of Spirit. It's old, made of wood and beautifully carved. The handle is made of gold, and is in the shape of a curving branch covered with leaves and berries. Grip the handle and pull. The door is heavy. Pull harder. It opens.

You stand amidst a softly swirling mist settling upon your skin like a soft cloak. Unable to see anything, not even the ground beneath your feet, you take a brave step forward. The mist sparkles, thins and evaporates. A rolling, lush and luminous green landscape appears, beneath your feet a carpet of green grass full of spring violets. The Sun is rising, the sky is blue and there's a soft warm breeze.

Inhale and fill yourself with the energy of this place. **Exhale and return it.** (Cue for Goddess and God visualizations ahead.)

A well-worn path appears before you, a stand of trees in the distance. Follow the path through a meadow and into the woods. The sunlight's brilliance softens. The air is filled with birdsong and the sounds of a tumbling stream. Walk toward the sound of the water, spiraled ferns unfurling as you pass them. You stop beside the stream, sitting on a moss-covered rock.

Watch the light bouncing in the dancing water. Feel the soft spray fall upon you, a blessing by holy waters. Breathe deeply. What do you smell? Damp earth? Flowers? Fallen leaves? Look around you. What do you see? What does the water look like, the light, the plants, the rocks? Look up: what do the trees look like, the sky above? Close your eyes. What do you hear? The wind? The stream? The birds? Is there singing? A voice speaking to you? Listen carefully.

Open your eyes. In front of you is a being of pure love and compassion. She may appear as a Goddess or a fairy; He as a God or Green Man. It may be an ancestor, a wise one, or other being of Spirit. They are your guide. Listen to their wisdom, to the blessing that you're being given. Open your heart and receive the gift they have for you. Whatever you need is offered. Listen carefully.

Close your eyes and feel their touch on your heart. Feel the blessing entering you, the energy coursing through you to every cell in your body. Feel the energy of Creation coursing through you, the creative force that made you, that made the world and all the living beings of this world and all the other worlds, that made the cosmos and all the places between the worlds to which you have now been granted access.

Fill yourself with the energy of life, the energy of this place, of Spirit. Feel the love and beauty and joy that is the energy of Creation. Feel the gift of your being. You can create anything that you wish with this energy, this life you've been given.

Your body is infused with light and energy, love and Spirit. There's something in your hands, something that you've shaped from this energy. It's a gift from you that your heart has created, an offering of thanks for what you've received. Give it to your guide and thank them.

Your time together, for now, is coming to an end. The shimmering mist swirls around your guide and they are gone.

It's time to return. Feel your heart beating, hear my words carry you back past the stream, out of the woods, along the path through the meadow, and through the door, which you close behind you. Back into the room, into your body, into the present. Feel your body; wiggle your fingers and your toes.

You have returned with the power of Creation to manifest love and beauty, to give shape and form to Spirit, to create the life that you long for. This is the magic you're seeking. When you're ready, open your eyes and sit up. Clap your hands three times to help you ground and return your consciousness to normal. Experience yourself fully present and back in your body and the room. Rest in the feelings and write about them in your magical journal.

Journeying

I want to share one of my favorite, most dependable practices and an essential part of my personal work and my tradition's: journeying. It has transformed the way in which I practice and teach Wicca; it has transformed my spirit and my life.

Journeying is one of the most ancient, universal and powerful shamanic techniques for gaining access to Spirit realms, non-ordinary reality, and much more. The form I use and share here comes from core shamanism, an essential and universal practice without a cultural overlay. That means you can add cultural specifics if and when you wish to and you'll be comfortable in other spiritual cultures that use drumming and journeying.

Many Euro-Indigenous cultures – including the Celts, Scandinavians, Sami, Gauls, Egyptians, Greeks and Romans – used drums and rattles to create an altered, ecstatic state. Journeying uses shamanic drumming, or in some traditions, rattles, click sticks or other percussive instruments, to 'hack' the brain, literally changing our consciousness. Studies have found that shamanic drumming, approximately 200 beats a minute, alters brain waves from beta, daily survival mode, to theta, a visionary state in which you're able to perceive and participate in other dimensions and realms of Spirit that you can't in normal awareness.

Shamanic consciousness is a capacity that's been part of you since you were born: you haven't realized it was missing because it hasn't been part of our culture for hundreds of years and you haven't been using it. Now you can cultivate your abilities and you're going to discover worlds of wonder. And you'll encounter spirit beings residing there who'll work with you to achieve healing, wisdom, power and other help and blessings.

There's a key to journeying: you need a guide who is your companion, guardian and teacher. In many shamanic traditions, your guide is usually a power animal – generally wild, not domesticated. Wiccans have always had animal guides and helpers in this and the Other realm, including animal companions like the Witch's familiar. Often depicted as a cat, a familiar can be any animal with whom you've cultivated a deep, spiritual relationship.

Many pre-Abrahamic deities had totemic animals of power, like Cybele's lions, Athena's owl, Hecate's pig, dog and horse, the Morrigan's ravens, Taliesen's salmon and Odin's horse. Or, like Herne the stag-antlered God and Sekhmet the lion-headed Goddess, they were themselves part animal.

Your guide can also be a spirit being, an ancestor, a sage or elder being, or a Euro-Indigenous spirit being like a fairy, elf or giant, or a mythological creature like a dragon, phoenix or mermaid. Or an angel. Whatever form it takes, your guide knows everything you need in order to journey safely and productively, and to lead a life filled with magic and blessings. Your first journey will be to find your guide, or power animal, and to spend time together. If you already journey, please journey for a new animal/guide or for the help you need.

Recordings of shamanic drumming are available online. Shamanic drumming requires mastery and skill, and so I recommend Dr. Michael Harner's CD, *Shamanic Journey Solo and Double Drumming*; you can also visit my website, www.phylliscurott.com. A shamanic drumming session lasts approximately 20 minutes.

Practice: Journey to find your power animal

Important: Read all of the below first, as you cannot read while journeying.

Set up the following things in a quiet place where you won't be disturbed: A **blanket** on the floor that you can lie on (plus another nearby to cover yourself if you get chilly; your **magical journal and a pen**; some **white sage** and something heavy in which to burn it; a **candle**, placed in a holder or dish, to provide light if you need it; **matches**.

There are just a few don'ts for journeying:

1. Don't eat garlic or drink alcohol beforehand.

2. Don't journey without your power animal/guide (except the first time, when you are finding them).

3. Don't go near reptiles and insects that appear on your journey. Some people do find that turtles, non-poisonous snakes, certain lizards, butterflies, bees or ladybugs (ladybirds) come to them as helpers. If, however, they bare their teeth or disturb you in any way, they are *not* your power animal.

4. Don't bring anything back with you.

5. Don't worry if nothing happens: you can do it again any time, or use another method, like a guided visualization or dream, to connect with your power animal. Be patient with yourself.

6. Don't second-guess your experience.

Let's begin.

Light the candle and turn off the lights. Purify yourself and the space. The traditional way to do this is to burn some white sage (you can buy this online, or use regular dried kitchen sage). Native Americans call this 'smudging'; sage was also used in Euro-Indigenous traditions as a cleansing herb. Carry the burning sage around the room in a circle, moving clockwise, and pass the smoke over and around yourself. Set the sage safely aside.

Lie down and cover your eyes with the scarf. Cover yourself with the blanket if you need to. Breathe and relax. Now turn on the drumming CD/recording. State the purpose for your journey, out loud or to yourself: *'I am journeying to find my power animal or spirit guide.'* Relax and don't second-guess what happens next.

Visualize an opening in the Earth. It can be a hole in the trunk or at the roots of a tree, a cave opening or an animal's burrow. It may be a place that you know and have visited, or one that you're simply imagining. Enter. There will be a tunnel opening up in front of you that pitches downward. Allow the drumming to help you move through it. You may walk or find yourself sliding. You'll see a light up ahead. This is the end of the tunnel and the opening to non-ordinary reality. When you reach this opening, leave the tunnel and enter non-ordinary reality.

You'll probably find yourself in a very beautiful natural landscape. Stay where you are. Call out the reason for your journey: *'I am here to find my power animal, my spirit guide.'* Wait patiently. It may happen immediately or take some time.

One animal may appear or many. You'll know your power animal is yours because it presents itself to you at least four times, or is very clear and insistent that it's your animal. If it's a spirit being, it will probably be the only one to appear and will make its purpose clear. When you're sure that this is your power animal/guide, embrace it.

You may feel as if it has entered your body, or you may feel yourself entering its body. (This is how shamans shape-shift – a skill for which *wicce* are famous, and one you'll cultivate.) Spend time together.

When the drumming stops and you hear a group of very fast beats repeated four times, you're being signaled to return. Thank your animal/guide, tell them you'll return and ask them to be with you and guide you in ordinary reality.

Return to the tunnel opening in non-ordinary reality. Drumming will begin again at an accelerated pace. Enter the tunnel and return to ordinary reality. The journey ends when you again hear four groups of fast beats. Take some deep breaths. Open your eyes. Stretch. Sit up. Write down in your magical journal what you experienced and any wisdom teaching you received from your animal/guide.

It's unlikely, but if you don't feel fully back, go back to the signal to return and play the fast drumming again. Sit up, stand up, turn on the lights, write.

You may also wish to put the drumming on again and *dance* your animal – literally welcoming it into your body as it expresses its joy in being with you. Move as you imagine your animal moves and soon and very naturally you'll feel it move with you. (This is also a first step in learning how to shape-shift.)

The next time you're going to journey, purify, put on the drumming recording and 'dance your animal' first. When you feel it's with you, lie down and journey into non-ordinary reality. State the purpose of your journey and call your animal to you. Once it arrives, it will guide you where you need to go and to what you need to learn, receive, etc.

Gratitude, and your relationship with your guide

It's important that you know that the animal, or guide, that comes to you is the one that you need now. It has the powers, wisdom and gifts that will best help you at this time. One of my students, a great big burly guy called Jack, was very disappointed, and embarrassed, when he got a chipmunk rather than the grizzly bear he thought suited him. But that chipmunk had precisely the skills, knowledge and magic that Jack needed and their relationship empowered his life.

In time, you may find other power animals or guides. My primary relationship is still with my first power animal, but I've acquired several others, each one arriving with just what I needed at the time, and my gratitude to them is profound. It's important to express your gratitude. I make offerings in the form of donations to organizations devoted to protecting my animals and their environments. I also cultivate our relationship by journeying regularly to work with them, dancing them, and finding ways to do the things they love outside in Nature. And I have statues and images of them on my altar, in my office, and objects I work with that hold their power.

You may find your animal/guide appearing in your life in all sorts of unexpected ways, especially when you need them. Record these encounters in your magical journal. It's up to you whether you tell people what your animal/ who your guide is, but whether you do or not, you may find people spontaneously giving you statues, cards and stuffed versions of them. Whenever I'm in someone's home and they have a huge collection of some animal, I know that animal has been a protective spirit watching over them.

As you work, you'll also develop a group of spirit helpers – these may include the spirits of plants, elemental beings and others who have special purposes and gifts in working with you for healing, divination or other specific purposes.

Doubt

Journeying is simple and easy, but like meditation, it may take some practice to stop your internal chattering and judging. You just have to relax and allow it to work. I want to reassure you if, at first, you doubt the reality of what you experience.

One of my very first journeys was for someone in the drumming circle who was a stranger, although I'd liked her on first sight. My journey was vivid, though a bit disjointed as I moved from one confusing scene to another. Toward the end, I encountered an old woman who told me her name and gave me a symbol and some very specific messages to deliver.

When we returned, everyone shared his or her journey, and I sat there silently, thinking I'd imagined it all. But everyone encouraged me, and so I described what I'd seen. It all made perfect sense to the woman for whom I was journeying, and when I told her the name of the old woman, she knew immediately who it was – a friend who had died months before – and the symbols and messages I'd been given for her were deeply meaningful. It was extraordinary: a blessing for her *and* for me because I realized that non-ordinary reality *was* real.

Many students worry that what they are experiencing isn't real. One of the gifts of working with others is that people return from journeying with similar experiences, helping everyone to have confidence in themselves and the technique. But even on your own, you'll see how the advice and help you're given in non-ordinary reality are invaluable in your ordinary life.

People describe their experiences differently. For some, it's like watching a movie. Others feel as if they're actually present in the world they've entered. Some say it's like virtual reality, and for others it's dreamlike and surreal. Sometimes the experience is very coherent and linear and other times it's erratic, with random images, colors or sounds. Sometimes you journey easily, other times it simply doesn't happen.

Don't judge and don't worry if you find it difficult to journey. For many years, one of my dearest and oldest friends, who is one of the world's greatest teachers of core shamanism, had a hard time journeying. Instead, she drummed for everyone else. Then one day, she entered the tunnel and found herself in non-ordinary reality.

As you work, you'll explore the realms of Spirit: the different levels of non-ordinary reality called the Lower, Middle and Upper worlds. To find your power animal/ guide, you journeyed in the Lower World, which has nothing to do with the Western Underworld. Be patient, be persistent and be attentive. Journeying is a profound spiritual practice that will change the way you view reality. It will change the way you live. It will change *you*.

A world of Spirit

In the past, people used journeying for practical purposes – to help them find shelter, water or game, or to diagnose illnesses and to learn which plants would cure them. It was also used to heal the wounds of psyches and to retrieve lost souls, to help the spirits of those who had died to cross over to Spirit and to visit with ancestors.

You can and should journey to help yourself with healing, both physically and emotionally, for guidance in making major life decisions – like finding a place to live, a new job or someone to love – to visit with a departed love one and much more. And because shamanism has always been a healing and helping practice, as soon as you feel more confident and skilled, you can and should journey for others. The technique is the same: you simply state the purpose of your journey when you emerge into non-ordinary reality and ask your power animal or guide to assist you.

We alter our consciousness and begin to alter reality. Change yourself and you change the world – in ways that are genuinely magical and utterly practical. Storytelling, journeying and other practices are also extraordinary techniques for experiencing the spirits and divinity that reside in the natural world, and Nature is where we'll discover and awaken magic next.

Chapter 5

Nature

Creation embodies Spirit.

Like the shamans and wicce before you, you'll return from Spirit realms with countless blessings and gifts. One of the most precious is the gift of sight – the ability to see the Sacred in the natural world all around you. Nature is revelation.

The 'mundane' world is an enchanted world because it's charged through with divinity. And with time and practice, like your shamanic ancestors, you'll learn to hear the plants speaking, the animals thinking and the universe singing, even when you're in so-called normal consciousness.

You'll be able to see the Sacred embodied by Nature. You'll also be able to see how you are part of Nature, and how your human nature is sacred.

Being in Nature

There are so many ways to discover the divinity of the natural world. The simplest is to spend time in Nature. It's an adventure worth ditching your phone for – it will awaken the divine magic within you.

I learned just how divinely alive Nature is on a winter camping trek into a remote canyon in Utah, one of the wildest places in the lower 48 states of the USA. My marriage was over, and so was any possibility of having children. My heart was broken, and so was my spirit. I thought this wilderness trip might help me heal. After just a few days in the barren landscape, and nights with punishing single-digit temperatures, I knew that without all the high-tech camping gear – clothes, subzero sleeping bag, water filter, matches and provisions – I would be dead.

Finally, the temperature warmed, and I went to sit on a high, sunny ledge. Slowly, the pain loosened its hold on my heart. I looked around myself, as if seeing for the first time, and there, high up on the sheer canyon wall, was a pictograph of an otherworldly figure crowned with a crescent Moon, or perhaps horns. Four thousand years ago, people lived in this wild canyon without any modern technology. Mother Earth fed them, gave them water and shelter and they not only survived, they created art, *mystical* art that is still here.

Hiking down between the canyon walls, it was as if I'd stepped into a field of energy. I knew that if I paid attention, Mother Earth would teach and provide me with whatever I needed to survive. For the remainder of my time within her womb, life showed itself to me – the wild donkeys that no one ever saw appeared every time I sang, tiny mice ran across my sleeping bag at night, and every day an eagle rode the thermals overhead. When I finally emerged, a message was waiting that the book deal I'd hoped and worked for had come through. My life was beginning again and I was ready.

Nature makes Spirit visible.

You don't have to trek into a wilderness canyon to experience Nature's divine power. But first you have to realize how much you need those experiences. Many of us don't recognize how drained of vitality we've become – we're benumbed by the constant bombardment of bad news and the deliberately addicting clicks, likes and responses of social media, and spend most of our lives indoors, literally suffering from Nature deficit disorder with anxiety, depression and attention disorders. Not to mention how disoriented our souls have become. We're living out of context, separated from the ground of being, from the natural world and the Sacred it reveals.

But the cure is right at hand. Studies have shown that we experience awe in places of natural beauty and that awe transforms us – our cortisol levels drop and our stress and aggression diminish. We become less egocentric, more generous, compassionate and optimistic. We become better human beings in Nature. Even if all you have is a backyard, a small city park, or the Sun coming in your window, Nature is always present, if you'll pay attention to your senses and open your heart.

Guided meditation: Come to your senses

You may want to record the text below, to listen to it outside, or simply read it through before you start. You'll need to take something with you as an offering – birdseed is always appreciated – and something to sit on.

Let's begin.

Find a spot outdoors in a natural setting that attracts or calls to you and where you won't be disturbed. A spot in your backyard, local park, or even an open window will do. Sit down, close your eyes, breathe deeply, and relax.

Bring your attention to your body. Notice how you're feeling – cold, warm, rested, tired, stiff? Breathe into the part of your body that draws your attention. Feel the improvement. Breathe until your entire body feels relaxed. Now bring you attention to one of your senses. Let's start with hearing. Listen to the sounds carried by the air. Pay attention. Are there distracting noises like traffic, machinery, airplanes, people's voices? Which directions are the sounds coming from? Do they stop and start? Is there a rhythm or music they create? Listen to the hum of humanity. Notice how it makes you feel.

Now open your eyes and look around you. Can you locate where the various sounds came from? When you feel ready, close your eyes again, and focus on the natural sounds. Let go of any distracting noise pollution, just as you've learned to let go of distracting thoughts when you meditate and journey. Bring your focus to the natural sounds. Listen carefully. Pay attention.

What do you hear? A bird? Different birds? A flock? Where are they? Are they talking to each other, as crows do? Are they singing? How do their songs make you feel? Do you hear the wind blowing, leaves rustling, trees whispering? Do you hear dogs barking? Do you hear bees or cicadas? Are you hearing sounds you've never noticed before? Is there a rhythm, a music, to Nature's sounds? Listen to the silence between sounds. How do you feel? If your mind starts to wander, return to being present in the moment by focusing on the sounds of Nature.

When you're ready, open your eyes. See if you can spot the sources of Nature's sounds. How does listening to Nature make you feel? How does it feel to come to your senses? Be sure to thank the place, its spirit, and leave your offering. Write about how you felt and what you experienced in your magical journal.

Over time, as you repeat this practice of sacred awakening, you may hear a song or poem, or some other expression of inspiration and wisdom. You may receive a gift of insight or a power song from the spirit of the place, the *genius loci*. You can use this same practice to develop your other senses – sight, smell, touch, even taste. Isolate each one of your senses and then concentrate on it, paying careful attention to your experience of the natural environment you're in.

Practice coming to your senses in this same spot at different times of the day and night, if it's safe to do so, and in different weather and different seasons. Pay attention to the differences in what you perceive. With time, each sense will become more acute and you'll become more aware of the other beings with whom you live, and more attuned to Nature's wisdom and blessings. The next time you're outdoors, or even watering a houseplant, notice how your body feels. Pay attention to what you're sensing and how present you're becoming.

Elemental magic

The more time you spend in Nature, the more embodied *your* spirit will become. But we're so cut off from the natural world that we forget Nature is not just the 'great outdoors,' limited to a vacation or an extreme wilderness trek. Working with the elements – Air, Fire, Water, Earth – helps you to recognize that Nature is everywhere, in everything, including you.

I was taught the old-fashioned approach to elemental magic, using Air, Fire, Water or Earth to bring about a desired change or outcome. It was fun and creative and sometimes it worked. But it took a long time to realize that there was a deeper magic waiting within the elements. You don't have to wait to discover that magic. It's where you're going to start.

Working with the elements is an active meditation, a spiritual practice that attunes you to the sacred wisdom and power of Nature: you discover how you and the Earth are interconnected and how you too are part of Nature. When you make magic with the elements, their energies help you to discover, transform and fulfill yourself. The elements show you how deity is present in the world and how these life-sustaining aspects of divinity are present in you. Each element is a part of you and the powers of the elements correspond to your powers.

Elemental magic makes you whole, unleashing an infinite flow of divine energies that move naturally into the corresponding areas of your life, with inspiration, transformation, healing, nourishment and more. You'll discover how your body and the body of Creation are one, your inner world and the outer world are one, your human nature and outer Nature are One, and how the magic that surrounds you is also within you. It's divine magic. It's natural magic.

The four elements

Each element is a physical *and* spiritual part of *you*.

❖ **Air** is the breath of life; it's also your mind, your intellect and intuition, your ability to be inspired and inspire.

❖ **Fire** is the generative energy of life; it's also your energy, willpower, passion, courage and ability to make changes.

❖ **Water** is the moistening fluid of life; it's also your emotions, your feelings and ability to love and dream.

❖ **Earth** is the food, flesh and bones of life; it's also your body, creativity, and your ability to grow, create and manifest.

Each element has gifts that will empower you:

Air magic

Use it for

Inspiration; creative thinking; thoughtfulness; ease of communication; peace of mind; remaining calm or focused; work involving your mind or communication, like learning, writing, lecturing, taking an exam; cultivating your intuition.

Ways to make Air magic

Breath; chant; meditate; write a poem, spell or invocation; journal; fly a kite with your spell written on it; breathe your prayer onto a feather that you tie to a tree for the spirits of Air to carry off; stand outside on a windy day and shout your affirmation; follow your intuition; say yes to everything for a day; create and use an incense.

Fire magic

Use it for

Power; change; transformation; courage; passion; determination; quick manifestation; purification; cleansing and banishing; enlightenment; illumination.

Ways to make Fire magic

Greet the Sun every morning; cook; burn a piece of paper on which you've written whatever you want to 'banish' – a spell to remove or get rid of a problem, bad habit or unwanted situation; carve a candle with your goal, place it on a plate and on your altar (more on this later), light it and let it burn until it's gone, cup your hands around the flame and draw its power into your belly – feel your power to make it manifest; build, tend and dance around an outdoor fire.

Water magic

Use it for

Love; dreams; to visit ancestors; to cultivate your intuition and your feelings; to help your emotions flow and change; to put out fires of conflict and anger; to cleanse and purify; to dissolve emotional blocks and heal emotional wounds; to nourish your inner landscape with self-love.

Ways to make Water magic

Create a potion and bathe in it; make an herbal tea and drink it; bathe, float, swim; go out in the rain and *get wet*; go whitewater rafting or sailing; jump into a deep body of water; water your garden; wash your face; stand at the edge of the ocean, where it rolls in and out of the shore's edge.

Earth magic

Use it for

Attuning to Nature's rhythms and cycles of birth, growth, death and rebirth; manifesting ideas and desires; cultivating creativity; creating prosperity; giving birth to the life you want; grounding, nourishing and taking care of your body and soul, to experience abundance.

Ways to make Earth magic

Put your hands in the dirt; plant a seed and nourish it, envisioning your goal growing as the plant grows; weed and envision that you're pulling up any problems, cares or obstacles; exercise and take care of your body; recycle your garbage; sit on the Earth and feel your heart beating; develop a relationship with a tree or other plant; ground (*see opposite*); walk your dog; cultivate a relationship with a natural spot as your place of power.

Earth magic

Let's look at the element of Earth with 'grounding' – the practice of running energy from Mother Earth through your body and back into Mother Earth. It's one of the most powerful and unique Wiccan techniques connecting you to Mother Earth and her divine life force that energizes, nourishes and heals all of life.

Practice: Grounding

You may want to record the following text, so you can listen to it as you practice. Grounding can be done indoors, but for maximum benefit you should work outside, seated directly on Mother Earth with your back against a tree. Take an offering, such as birdseed.

Let's begin.

Find a tree that you feel drawn to, where you can sit without being disturbed. Ask the tree for its help. The response may come with a sign, like the rustling of its leaves or a bird singing, or simply a feeling of joy and acceptance. Acknowledge and thank it, sit down with your back against its trunk and close your eyes.

Breathe, and when you feel yourself relaxed and peaceful, your awareness open and expanded, bring your attention to the life force coursing through the tree. Feel the power, energy and vitality giving this tree life. Sit up straight and feel your back becoming strong and solid, like the tree's trunk. Ask the tree to teach you what it's like to be a tree rooted in Mother Earth.

Exhale and feel yourself sending roots from the base of your spine down into Mother Earth beneath you. At first, you may need to 'imagine' this but very quickly you'll feel the sensation of your roots growing, pushing downward, connecting you to Mother Earth. Feel her beneath you, surrounding your roots, embracing them and holding them with love. Feel her accepting you with love and joy.

Exhale and feel your roots descending, expanding, stretching, reaching into the moist and nourishing Mother Earth. Feel your roots becoming thinner and finer, like thousands of tiny hairs, nestling into the love of Mother Earth.

Now inhale and feel her energy flowing into you. Feel the minerals and water, the nourishing life force flowing into you. Feel Mother Earth's energy coursing upward through your roots, up your spine, into all the nerves in your body, which branch outward like the tree that's supporting you. Feel her energy flowing up your spine, through your muscles, your organs, your consciousness. Inhale and draw up the energy of Mother Earth, the energy of the divine life force, into your body. Feel her energy rising up your spine, spreading through you, circulating through you, filling and energizing you.

Inhale and draw the energy up. Now direct the energy into whichever part of your body or spirit needs healing. Feel the warmth, the nourishment, the vitality flowing through and healing you. You may feel tingling, or sensations of love, light and potency. Feel yourself healed, nourished, strengthened. Breathe and feel yourself grounded in Mother Earth, rooted in Mother Earth, loved by Mother Earth. Feel your heart overflowing with joy, with life, with love. Hold the energy in your heart.

When you're ready, gently, slowly, gratefully withdraw your roots from Mother Earth. Feel them curling into themselves – the smaller ones merging with the larger roots, the larger roots moving slowly back up from the generous, life-generating Earth. Feel them curl neatly into the base of your spine. Take a deep breath. Thank Mother Earth and the tree for their blessings.

When you're ready, open your eyes. You may be dazzled by the beauty that you see. The tree and your own body may be glowing and you may see auras or energy radiating from everything around you. If you feel light-headed, put your palms and the bottoms of your feet on the ground and return the excess energies to Mother Earth and the tree that has helped you. Take your time. Leave your offering.

Reflect on your experiences in your magical journal – on what it feels like to develop a personal relationship with Mother Earth and how it changes the way you think and act.

You're mastering an important technique that will help you discover and deepen your relationship with Mother Earth, and one of her most precious children: the tree who is teaching you how to be grounded. (And is also an immortal, shamanic guide connecting this world with realms of Spirit.)

The Table of Correspondences

There are many ways of making elemental magic. An elegant system of meaning and symbols called the *Table of Correspondences* will help you make yours.

Some of this organizational system comes from the ancient Greeks, and is found in European esoteric and ceremonial magic, and some has been recently developed. It also reflects Euro-Indigenous wisdom, and parallels can be found in other Indigenous traditions elsewhere in the world.

Briefly, each of the four elements corresponds not only to human qualities *and* aspects of Nature, but also the four directions, times of day and seasons, elemental spirits, deities, animals, plants, colors, astrological signs, Tarot suits and more.

Table of Correspondences

Direction	East	South	West	North
Element	Air	Fire	Water	Earth
Nature	Wind, Breeze	Sun	Oceans, Rivers, Rain, Lakes	Mountains, Woods, Fields, Caves
Aspects	Mind, Know	Will, Dare	Heart/Womb, Feel	Body, Manifest
Qualities	Imagination, Intelligence, Intuition, Communication, Poetry, Music	Passion, Courage, Determination, Desire, Power, Transformation, Action	Love, Compassion, Emotions, Dreams, Ancestors, Reflection, Purification, Connection	Creativity, Fertility, Rebirth, Strength, Groundedness, Abundance, Generosity
Colors	White, Pale Blue, Lavender	Red, Orange, Yellow	Blue, Sea Green	Green, Gold, Brown, Purple
Symbol	Feather	Candle	Shell	Seed
Time	Dawn	Midday	Sunset	Midnight
Season	Spring	Summer	Autumn	Winter

Direction	East	South	West	North
Animal	*Wing*	*Claw*	*Fin*	*Paw, Hoof, Horn*
	Bird, Butterfly, Dragonfly	Lion, Dragon, Lizard	Dolphin, Whale, Otter, Fish	Bear, Wolf, Bison, Stag, Horse
Plant	Lavender, Bodhi Tree	Myrrh, Olive tree	St. John's wort, Willow	Patchouli, Oak
Tool	Sword, Athame	Wand	Cup, Cauldron	Pentacle, Stone
Astrological sign	Gemini, Libra, Aquarius	Aries, Leo, Sagittarius	Cancer, Scorpio, Pisces	Taurus, Virgo, Capricorn
Spirit form	Sylph	Salamander	Undine	Gnome
Goddess	Aurora, Isis, Arianrhod	Amaterasu, Brigid, Pele	Aphrodite, Yemaya, Tiamat	Demeter, Parvati, Freyja
God	Hermes, Thoth, Quetzalcoatl	Horus, Surya, Lugh, Sol	Poseidon, Njord, Agwe	Dionysus, Cernunnos, Osiris, Green Man

With time and practice, elemental correspondences will become a familiar vocabulary, an artist's palette rich with spiritual meaning. Each element offers a path of self-awareness, balance and fulfillment as you move around the sacred circle of your life. Working magically with each of the four elements, you learn how to discern and intuit, to have passion and courage, to love and heal, to cultivate and create.

There are many more aspects and qualities, animals and plants, Goddesses and Gods associated with each of the elements, but the Table of Correspondences (*see previous pages*) provides a few examples that you can begin to explore and work with.

Just as you will when casting circle, I recommend you begin with Air (East), then Fire (South); next work with Water (West) and finally Earth (North). As you meditate, reflect and begin to make magic with each of the elements, you'll discover where you're out of balance, and you'll learn how to restore equilibrium to all aspects of your Self, your inner and outer nature, your inner life and your outer expression.

For example, are your heart and mind out of balance? Are you too intellectual and out of touch with your feelings? Working with Water will release your emotions and open you to love. Are you too quick to anger? Working with Earth will channel your fiery-ness and teach you patience. Are you down in the weeds and unable to see the big picture? Working with Air will lift you up and clear your vision.

Working with the elements

Reflect on the meaning of each of the elements' qualities. Consider each element in terms of your strengths and weaknesses. Write down your findings in your magical journal:

❖ Which qualities do you have in abundance? Do you need more of a quality, or less?

❖ Which element is associated with those qualities? What are its correspondences? Do they resonate for you? In what ways can you bring an element's energies into your life?

❖ Which element will help create balance where you have too much or too little of a quality? How can you achieve greater balance within and harmony without?

You may know immediately, or it may take time to recognize yourself, your gifts and your gaps. What follows is a simple plan for engaging creatively and magically with the elements and gradually, organically, becoming balanced and whole, inside and out. And the Table of Correspondences will provide the essential information you'll need.

Practice: Making magic with Nature

Spend a month working with each element. Trust your intuition and your creativity. Reflect on the element's meaning in your life.

1. Create an altar devoted to the element placed in the corresponding direction (this will be different depending on whether you are in the Northern or Southern hemisphere).

    Use an altar cloth and candles of the appropriate color. Place the element and objects that symbolize the element in the center of your altar. Include statues and images of the animals and deities associated with the element. Create an incense, oil or potion using plants (herbs) associated with the element.

2. Work with the magical tool associated with the element. You don't need a chalice, a sword or a wand – your tools can come from your kitchen. You can use a wine glass, a kitchen knife and a tree branch.

3. Wear the colors of the element.

4. Learn about and learn from the Nature beings associated with the element: pay attention, use your intuition, alter your consciousness, listen with your heart.

5. Watch for signs of the element in Nature and in your immediate surroundings.

6. Write an invitation or invocation of the element to be present and to bless you. Some examples of how my Tradition of Ara honors the elements, and the four directions, are below.

7. Create a different way to make magic with the element each week. For example, for the element of Water, you're working with the gifts of the heart – emotions, dreams and visions. During the

month, pay attention to your feelings and your dreams and keep a dream journal.

❖ Your first Water magic might be a purification bath, the next a self-blessing with water. The third Water magic might be to 'charge' a bowl of water by placing it overnight beneath the light of a full Moon. Use the water to bless yourself, your working tools, your circle (more on both of these coming up), your home, a symbol of the dream you want to come true. Pour the remainder on a plant, with love.

❖ Or you could go swimming, or spend time in a flotation tank. Float an offering on nearby waters to a Goddess or God of the sea or simply to the waters themselves with thanks for their blessings. Journey to meet and work with the Water elemental, an undine or creatures of Water like whales. Learn about your ancestors who rest in the West, the Wiccan direction that corresponds with Water.

❖ Learn about the Holy Grail and the Cauldron of Cerridwen – symbols of the Goddess and her generative powers of rebirth. Thank the Water before your first drink in the morning and when you get in the shower or bath.

Keep a record of your elemental magic, your experiences and reflections in your magical journal.

Meet and work with the elementals

One of my favorite practices is to cultivate my relationship with my place of power. It's a place of visions, healing, enlightenment, soul nourishment and magic. Your place of power doesn't have to be on a sacred mountaintop or in an ancient cave, although those places are charged with divinity and will work with you if approached with reverence and openness. Your backyard is filled with magic and grace and will offer its blessings if you ask, because all natural places have a spirit, called the *genius loci*.

There are also Nature spirits – the spirit of a particular plant or animal – and spirit beings of the elements, which are called elementals. You can journey to meet them, meditate or simply pay attention and respect your intuition as they communicate with you. If approached with respect, they will teach, help and heal you.

Practice: Finding your place of power and meeting the spirit of place

You can find your place of power simply by using your intuition.

Take a walk, pay attention, listen, feel, look, wander and wonder. And when you feel yourself drawn to a spot, a tree, a flower, a rock, a hollow, a stream, a place of natural beauty that beckons you, ask if it's your place of power. If you have that special feeling of joy, acceptance, comfort, you know you've found it.

Cultivating a relationship requires attention, effort and consistency. Try to visit your place of power regularly, clean it up, take water and other offerings, plant flowers or grass or whatever the place tells you it needs. Watch, listen and learn. Over time, you'll get to know the *genius loci*, the spirit of the place, and it will become your teacher, your companion, your guardian, as you'll become its.

Be patient if you don't meet the *genius loci* immediately. It can take time for them to trust us, given the terrible damage we've done to the natural world. Next time you visit your place of power, be sure to express your love for the spot and for Mother Earth. Share your sincere willingness to work together to heal and repair Mother Earth's wounded places. And bring an offering for the birds and animals. After you've met and begun working together, you can also ask for advice about your life, your spiritual journey, the challenges you face and goals you've set.

Working with the elements, you're healing your separation from Mother Earth and the Sacred that is the root of so many of the wounds we all suffer from. As you heal, the Earth heals.

Natural blessings

Below are four Invocations of the Elements, also called Honoring the Four Directions or the old term, Calling the Quarters. These are traditionally done at the beginning of casting circle, which you'll learn more about soon. Working with them now, especially when you do your month-long work with each element (*see Making magic with Nature practice on page 84*) will prepare you to use them when you cast circle.

Invocations of the Elements

Read the invocations aloud; repetition leads to memorization, and then use them as a model for writing your own. Begin by facing East, where the Sun rises, and recite the Honoring of Air, then turn to the South and address Fire. Turn to the West and speak to Water. Next, turn to the North and honor Earth and finally turn back to the East, because we always end where we began, completing the circle. You'll be amazed by how much you've changed.

East/Air

I call the ancient spirits of the East

Powers of Air

Where the Sun rises in the morning

Powers of wonder and imagination

Clarity and communication

Laughter, music, birds singing, breezes blowing

Blessings of eagle and butterfly

All creatures on the wing

I invite you to this sacred circle,

Hail and welcome! [this last phrase is traditional]

South/Fire

I call the ancient spirits of the South

Powers of Fire

Where the Sun is high in the midday sky

Powers of passion and determination

Courage and transformation

Light, energy, flames leaping, fire burning

Blessings of lion and dragon

All creatures of fang and claw

I invite you to this sacred circle,

Hail and welcome!

West/Water

I call the ancient spirits of the West

Powers of Water

Where the Sun sets and our ancestors dwell

Powers of love and dreaming

Compassion and healing

Womb, water, oceans flowing, rain falling

Blessings of whale and otter

All creatures of fin and those who swim

I invite you to this sacred circle,

Hail and welcome!

North/Earth

I call the ancient spirits of the North

Powers of Earth

Where the Mystery dwells

Powers of fertility and creation

Rebirth, strength and manifestation

Seed, mountain, forest knowing, fields growing

Blessings of bear and wolf and stag

All creatures of fur and paw, hoof and horn

I invite you to this sacred circle,

Hail and welcome!

The more you practice any Wiccan technique, the simpler and easier it becomes and the deeper the experiences you'll have. My own morning ritual in my garden, addressing each direction and scattering birdseed as I turn in a circle, goes something like this: 'May my thoughts be clear, may my determination hold fast, may my heart be open, may my work be of value. May I be aware and grateful today.' And I am.

Spirit embodied

John Muir, one of America's greatest naturalists, observed that 'every natural object is a conductor of divinity.' Nature gives Spirit its form. It makes Spirit knowable. And just as it was for our Indigenous ancestors, it's our greatest spiritual teacher. The more time you spend in Nature, the clearer it will become that Nature doesn't just nourish our bodies. It nourishes our souls.

One of the most profound lessons Nature has taught me is that Creation reveals a divine blueprint, a sacred order. And Nature has a holy magic we must rediscover: all life – rabbit, hummingbird, mushroom, whale, every living thing – cares for the world that's taking care of it.

**Whatever Nature's children do to live –
eat, make a home, procreate, recreate,
evacuate – makes the place where
they live, the Earth where they live,
more conducive for *all* Life.**

Only human beings have forgotten.

But everything we need to remember, to live a healthy, abundant and joy-filled life that makes the world a better place for all, is right here – within us and all around us. Working with the elements you discover that just as Mother Earth is the embodiment of the Divine, so are you. Elemental magic heals our separation from essential parts of ourselves, from Nature and divinity. The boundary between inner and outer drops and a profound flow of divine energy, love and blessings begins. You're becoming whole and your spirit is becoming fully embodied in your life.

You're mastering the methods of an embodied spirituality, a path guided by Nature's deep spiritual intelligence, a path back home to a world charged through with divinity and a life charged through with divinity – mind, spirit *and* body. You're becoming one with Creation. You're awakening the divine magic within.

Chapter 6

Casting Circle

It's midnight, the proverbial Witching hour. Alone in my garden, I reach out to the full Rose Moon rising through the trees, take it into my hands and bring it to my heart. I inhale deeply, hearing the night's music more clearly. I close my eyes and feel the lunar light glowing within.

Time disappears, and when I open my eyes, the Moon shines above the treetops, bathing the world in silver. I'm already facing East, where Sun and Moon both rise. Inhaling, I thank the trees for the breath of life. Exhaling, I return the gift to them.

Slowly, I turn clockwise to the South, knowing the Moon shines with the fire of the unseen Sun. I turn again, to the West, and feel the tidal waters where I live and that live in me pulled closer together by the Moon. I turn clockwise again, to the North, to the direction of Mother Earth, and feel her ever-present support beneath my bare feet.

> *The Great Bear watches over me from above as I turn one last time, back to the East, ending where I began. I lift the Moon from my heart and return her to the sky above me. Grateful for the privilege of my life, I bend and touch Mother Earth beneath me. My circle is cast. I am between the worlds where Spirit and Nature are One.*

Sacred circles

The circle is ancient – an essential spiritual element of most Indigenous cultures. Circles are an evocation of Creation and its eternal cycles. It's a space we create, we conjure, we recognize already exists. We step inside a circle and step outside the limits of time and space. Within circle, we return to the Sacred and become whole. It's the safe and sacred space for ceremony and healing, transformation and magic and communion.

The process of creating a circle, of 'casting circle' as Wiccans say, is simple, the meaning layered, the occasion profound. The very first thing that happens when you cast circle is the opening of your awareness and your heart. Initially, you may feel awkward or uncertain, or you may feel no difference at all. But gradually, self-consciousness is replaced by being present, resistance gives way to rejoicing and any worries about 'doing it right' are replaced by spontaneity.

Like meditation, journeying, grounding and other Wiccan practices, casting circle changes your consciousness.

I feel it the minute I begin and, in time, you will too. Casting also initiates the flow of divine energies. Even the first time, you'll feel the extraordinary power moving through you and, if you're with others, everyone in the circle. It can be startling, releasing deep emotions and dissolving defenses, but circle is always a safe space. And like the other spiritual practices you're mastering, when you let go and focus on being present in the moment, in the *experience*, divinity becomes present – in you and in circle – and magic follows.

> **The process of casting circle awakens**
> **the Sacred within and creates a temple**
> **for the Sacred that surrounds us.**

The Circle and Goddess

Goddess Circle Goddess Circle Goddess Circle
Goddess Circle Goddess...

Circle is a prayer that is answered. It's a symbol of the Sacred Feminine dating back to the Paleolithic period, a first sign of human consciousness and fascination with the Mysteries of Creation. To gather in circle for any sacred purpose is to invoke the Sacred Feminine, the Goddess. And whether they are aware of it or not, as soon as people sit together, take hands, offer thanks in a circle, the Goddess is present. (We'll explore all this in Chapter 7.) It is Her wisdom, energy and blessing that you will experience.

Circle embodies the Goddess. You feel nourished, protected and surrounded by love because you are within the womb of the Great Mother Goddess. This is the blessing power of circle. Immersed within this sacred space, we're one with the divine life force from which all of Creation is shaped and the Source from which it flows. When circle is 'closed' or 'opened' (these words are used interchangeably to mean ended), we return to the world transformed and empowered to create the lives we're here for.

The magical cauldron

The Celtic Goddess Cerridwen had a magical cauldron of wisdom and rebirth: it is the mythological origin of the Witch's cauldron and a symbol of the womb of Creation. Circles are cauldrons where you make the magic that changes you and your life. It's an alchemical vessel where your soul is awakened and your struggles and sorrows, doubts and damages are transformed into illumination, compassion and power.

The most common explanation for why we cast circle is to create a container to hold the energy we work with in making magic, just as you need a pot in which to boil water. It may sound like a fairy tale, but it's a *physical* phenomenon that you'll experience. The first time I learned this lesson was shortly after my Initiation in the very first circle I cast for strangers.

It was late at night, outdoors in New Hampshire, and hours had passed within our circle as we honored the season's change, offered libations, shared stories and laughed a lot. We were warm and comfortable and suddenly we were freezing. Someone had left the circle and when he came back, he admitted he'd forgotten to 'cut out,' a simple way to preserve the integrity of the circle by opening and closing 'a door' in its circumference. He'd broken the container and in an instant, all the heat rushed out. As you work, even alone, the temperature within a circle rises and drops when circle is ended.

Moving energy

All energy moves in a circular manner. From the invisible quantum level of subatomic particles whirling in their orbits to vast galaxies spinning in theirs, the universe moves in circles. Within circle, you work with the natural movement of energy.

To manifest or create, we move *deosil*: the direction of the Sun's 'movement' across the sky, clockwise or left to right in the Northern Hemisphere and counterclockwise right to left in the Southern. This is also the movement of increase. We move *widdershins* to decrease the energy, for banishing, purification or some kinds of healing work – this is counterclockwise in the Northern Hemisphere and clockwise in the Southern.

Like stirring ingredients in a bowl or a pot, moving in one direction within the circle is the most efficient and natural way to work with the organic flow of energy. That's how real magic works – learn from Nature and work with the natural movement of energy. We live within the eternal circle of Creation, the cycles of life and seasons, Moon and Sun, tides and the turning stars above us. And their cadences are ours. Circle attunes our souls to the divine rhythms of the cosmos and the natural world in which we live. The effect really is magical: shifting and enhancing your perception, your energy and your capacities. We'll talk more about this eternal circle dance in Chapter 9, The Wheel of the Year.

Sacred space

Casting circle is often described as creating sacred space. What does that really mean? Let's start with the sacred spaces we're already familiar with. The dominant patriarchal religions of the West conduct worship in churches, temples or mosques at an appointed time. The worship space reflects the cosmology and its power dynamics: worshippers (mostly passive) sit or kneel in rows while the spiritual professional, usually or exclusively male, presides on a raised platform from which rites, prayers and offerings are led, and is in turn subordinate to a Father God far above. The structure of church, temple or mosque reflects the power relationships and the energy dynamics of patriarchy.

Wicca doesn't require a building or an ordained deputy in order to experience the presence of divinity, and neither do you. Cast circle and you're in sacred space. Lay a circle of stones upon Mother Earth, step within it and you're in sacred space. Stand beneath the circling stars above and you're in sacred space. Spread out your arms, spin slowly round and you're at the center of the circle of an entirely holy universe.

Circles also express a very different spiritual perspective and social relationship. The physical shape – the roundness – embodies the Goddess. There are crones and elders, Priestesses and Priests who conduct ceremony and are respected as spiritual teachers and leaders, but there's no elevated podium separating them from the community. Their principal role is not to interpret or intercede, but to facilitate. Within circle, there's no hierarchy between you and the Divine.

Everyone is essentially equal in circle, and everyone's energy, presence and contribution is important. Just as cooking pots are round to provide equal distribution of heat, a circle distributes divine energy equally throughout the practitioners, though each of us responds in uniquely personal ways. It's also meaningful that we see one another in circle, look into each other's eyes and experience our interconnection. Even with hundreds of people, circle creates community, especially as we discover that the energy that creates, circulates and sustains all circles is love.

Your circle

You can cast circle anywhere – in your home, garden, place of power, in Nature, at a sacred site or in the Other World. It's your consecrated sacred space. It's wonderful to be able to dedicate a space in your home, but many of us don't have this luxury, so we cast circles in our living room, bedroom or backyard. Be sure to purify the space first, which also purifies and prepares you, and always properly close (open) or 'banish' your circle when done. Electronic equipment is particularly sensitive to accumulating magical energy.

As I'm writing about *your* circle, hawk has landed in the middle of mine. Protected by old, curving boxwood bushes, it's a beautiful area in my backyard where I've worked for more than 16 years. Hawk reminded me to share that when you cast circles in the same place, over time the place will 'hold a charge.' You feel it when you visit ancient sacred sites. And as it happens, hawks and foxes and other Nature beings, spirits and deities will abide there, with you. They will also come because a circle is a portal between the worlds. That's how I met the Green Man who appeared at the center of a sacred circle in Italy. Within circle, you are able to move outside the limits of time and space. You can travel to the Other World, to realms of Spirit, return to the past and past lives, visit with ancestors, move ahead into the future and change it. You can meet spirit helpers and the manifestations of deity that enter your sacred space. You can make magic.

Cast your circles and gradually you'll begin to
see that you're not really creating sacred space.
Rather, you'll discover the sacredness of the
space you already inhabit. That is a profound
shift in awareness and that is real magic.

Your altar

The altar is where Spirit and Earth are One. Magically,
it's the center of the universe, and most often it's placed
at the center of the circle. It's also a focal point for daily
spiritual practice, for reflection, meditation and magic. In
my garden circle, it's a beautiful round iron table where
hawk just landed.

An altar can be a permanently dedicated surface or it can
be temporary – a small table consecrated just for use as
your altar, or a coffee table you clear off and purify when
you're ready to cast circle; a shelf on your bookcase or
the top of your dresser; a cloth on the ground; a large
piece of stone, or a tree trunk that becomes your place
of power. I love creating community altars with people
– they are stunning, creative and impermanent works
of sacred art. Like a Buddhist mandala or Navajo sand
painting, an altar can be created as an active meditation,
prayer or offering, and then 'swept away.'

If there's space and time, setting up elemental altars
in each of the four directions helps you master the
Correspondences and is a focal point for your elemental
magic.

Practice: Making a personal altar

Creating a personal altar, whether it's temporary or permanent, is an empowering chance to express your sacred self. There's a traditional, basic design for Wiccan altars and the placement of magical/ritual tools, the four elements or symbols of them, statues and natural objects that embody Goddess and God and non-gendered divinity, seasonal decorations, candles and personal objects of power.

Below is a diagram of the design that you can follow to set up your own altar. In Chapter 11 you'll learn about the traditional power objects and ritual tools it shows. In the meantime, your altar can be as simple as a candle in a bowl of water – which naturally symbolizes the union of polarity, the fertilizing light of the Sun/God and the life-generating womb of the Earth/Goddess – surrounded by fruit and flowers. Whatever you choose to place on your altar, make it beautiful.

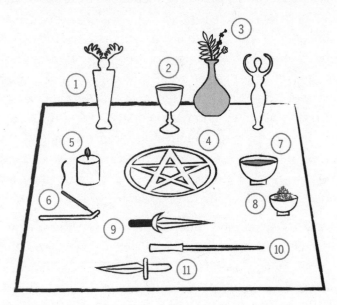

Key to objects and tools

1. Statues of Gods and Goddesses
2. Goddess chalice/bowl/cup
3. Flowers/natural objects
4. Pentacle
5. Candle (fire)
6. Incense (air)
7. Water in a bowl/shell (water)
8. Salt/seeds in a bowl (earth)
9. Athame
10. Wand
11. White hilt knife

I also have a permanent personal altar inside, and one outside that lives a double life. Don't neglect your altar if you leave it up; it deserves daily devotion and care that's as simple as giving thanks (see below) and keeping it tidy.

Above all, an altar must speak *from* your heart and *to* your heart. It's your expression of the Sacred and your offering to divinity in whatever shape and form that's meaningful for you. You may wish to create an altar to a specific deity that you're working with or that's become your patron deity, a wonderful way to learn about and interact with that deity.

Your altar is a place for meditation, reflection, divination; for writing in your magical journal and making magic. It's a place for the magic of charging jewelry, a project you're working on, a symbol, talisman, a work of art, or other objects of meaning and power, or even something like a 'wishboard.' You can also make an altar devoted to your ancestors, or for a specific magical effort or personal transformation you're undertaking, like finding your soul's purpose, a new job or a new love. (We'll explore this further in Chapter 10.)

A final important point about you and altars: as I explained earlier, the name of my tradition, Ara, means altar in Latin. It's said that long ago the Priestess *was* the altar. Today, we understand that each of *us* is an altar. *You* are the altar. You are Spirit and Earth conjoined, the divine magic of divinity living in the world.

Casting circle

Now that you understand the reasons *why* we cast circle, let's look at *how* to cast circle. Below are the essential steps, followed by a detailed guide to help you understand what to do, what to say, where to stand and even how to gesture at key points. Feel free to use the text below. With repetition you'll memorize it, and ultimately you may find yourself speaking from your heart. You can also see how I set up an altar and cast circle in my YouTube video, 'How to Set Up a Wiccan Altar' (*see Resources for more information*).

Take your time and don't worry if you leave out a step, confuse a direction or forget words. Very often there's some magical message or humor in the 'mistake.'

Mastery takes time and practice, but this is a spiritual discipline of joy and the experiences you have will encourage you to keep practicing. Remember, if you work it, it will work! Cast circle once a week, and you'll be amazed at how quickly you master the method and experience the magic.

Practice: Casting circle step by step

1. Purify and cleanse yourself and your space.

2. Set up your altar.

3. Purify and consecrate the space.

4. Cast circle – use one of the two methods described below.

5. Breathe – before or after casting.

6. Ground – before or casting.

7. Honor the Directions (opening the 'portal' for the elementals).

8. Honor/Invoke the Sacred/Goddess/God.

9. State the purpose or intent of the circle.

10. Make magic, working with/running/moving divine energy:

    ❖ Grail – open yourself to receive divine energy to charge your intention and magic.

    ❖ Wand – raise energy from within and the Earth to manifest your intention and magic.

11. Offer libation/wisdom discerned and share cakes/bread.

12. Thank the Sacred/Goddess/God.

13. Thank each of the four directions (close the elemental portals).

14. Close circle (also called 'open circle').

15. Put away your altar.

A guide to casting circle

1. Purify and cleanse your space

Always begin by purifying yourself and your space. Take a bath or shower, or wash your hands and face. You can burn a cleansing herb like white sage or scatter salt water around the circumference of your circle. This step begins to shift your attention from daily distractions to being present in the moment and with the Sacred.

2. Set up your altar

Enjoy the creativity and beauty of setting up your altar. Place whatever items you need to work with under or beside it, including something for your libation (step 11). Take a few minutes to breathe and ground (steps 5–6). You can also do these after casting circle. You'll begin to feel your heart opening, your perception shifting and the Earth's energy moving through you.

3. Purify and consecrate with the elements

Traditionally, the next step is to purify and consecrate the elements on the altar. Since Nature *is* divine, I no longer purify the elements. It's the elements that can help *us* to purify and consecrate ourselves and our circles.

Use each of the elements to purify yourself and the space. The simplest way to bless and consecrate yourself and others with each of the elements is to touch them or pass them before your third eye, your heart and your groin. The circle is then purified, blessed and consecrated as each element, beginning with Air, then Fire, Water and finally Earth, is carried, *deosil*, once around the circle, beginning and ending in the East.

4. Cast circle

The next important step is the demarcation of the circle's perimeter, which is also the specific step called 'casting circle.' You are literally creating a boundary, like the walls of a vessel, within which the energy will be contained.

Method 1

Casting with a wand, athame, sword, or hand

In British Traditional Witchcraft like the Gardnerian and Alexandrian traditions, as well as many new and eclectic Wiccan traditions, this step is usually done by the Priestess or Priest circling the perimeter of standing or seated participants, or the altar if one is alone, using a wand, an athame or a sword (you'll learn about these 'power objects' in Chapter 11).

Use Method 1 when you cast circle by and for yourself; but don't worry, you don't need a ritual tool to cast circle – you can use your hand, a tree branch, a feather, a flower: anything from Nature that appeals to you and extends your reach. You can also cast by standing in front of your altar at the center of the circle and turning *deosil* (Northern Hemisphere clockwise, Southern Hemisphere counterclockwise), three times.

❖ A circle is traditionally 9ft (2.8m) across and marked on the ground, but don't worry about the size or marking it on the floor. Just raise your hand or whatever you're using before you and walk *deosil* around your altar (or the outside of the circle of participants if you're working with others).

❖ Begin in the East, acknowledge the direction, walk slowly *three times* around the circle and end where you began. Why the East? Because this is where the Sun rises.

❖ As you walk, visualize a circle of light flowing from the tips of your fingers, or whatever you're using. Gradually, you'll be able to *feel* the energy rising from the Earth and flowing through you, creating the circle as you walk. Take your time.

❖ In the beginning, cast silently and keep your focus on feeling the energy as you cast. If you don't feel it, continue to visualize it. Later, you can add a spoken invocation.

Below is a variation on Method 1 that blends the traditional style with its poetically archaic language, with elements of my tradition's more shamanic approach. It's difficult to read, walk *and* feel the energy, so when you're ready to speak, memorize it. Don't worry about forgetting or making mistakes. When you're ready, write your own words, and ultimately you'll speak spontaneously from your heart.

❖ The first time around the circle say: *'I cast this circle as a sacred space, a place between the worlds where the worlds meet.'*

❖ The second time around the circle, say: *'I conjure this circle to contain the energies that I (we) shall receive and raise herein.'*

❖ The third time, say: *'I consecrate this circle as a safe and sacred place where Spirit and Earth are one, in perfect love and perfect trust.'*

❖ Stop in the East, where you began, and declare, *'Circle is cast. We are/I am between the worlds!'*

❖ See the light you've spun around the circle spreading into a sphere surrounding you and the entire area with energy. Remain facing East because...

But first, let's return to casting circle with Method 2.

Method 2

Casting circle hand to hand

This is the method I prefer when casting with more than one person because everyone participates. It connects us all and is very moving, emotionally and energetically.

♦ Everyone sits or stands together in a circle. Whoever is sitting in front of the altar begins, traditionally the Priestess or Priest, or you as the person who is leading or facilitating the circle. Turn to the person on the left, make eye contact and smile. Take your neighbor's right hand in your left and say: *'Hand to hand I cast this circle.'*

♦ This second person now turns to the person on her left, takes his hand, makes eye contact, hopefully smiles and says: *'Hand to hand I cast this circle.'*

♦ This continues all around the circle until everyone is holding hands. You, as the person who began, concludes by saying: *'Hand to hand and heart to heart, we cast our circle. And so we remember where we are and why we are here.'* Whenever someone ends with these words, you know you're working in the Ara Tradition.

A helpful note: As you take hands (see previous steps), everyone keeps their thumbs to the left. This helps the flow of energy – each person will have their left hand, their heart hand, cupped palm up and their right hand palm down. It's a way of offering energy from a posture that evokes the Goddess. Everyone should speak so they can be heard and everyone should make eye contact. Extra magic points for smiling!

5-6. Breathe and Ground

Along with chanting, which we've explored already, and sharing or 'running,' i.e. moving the energy through the circle, these are very powerful. People are often feeling group energy for the first time. A simple *Om* that begins, builds and ends spontaneously is a powerful way for people to feel their energies blending. Or you can use one of the many Wiccan chants, some of which you'll find throughout this book.

Running or moving energy is a simple but powerful practice that also connects everyone in the circle to each other, to the green plants and to the Earth itself. I guide people in moving energy by asking them to ground and bring the energy up from the Earth and run it through their bodies, holding it in their hearts.

Next, I ask them to exhale and send the energy down from their heart through their left arm and palm to the person on their left. Then we all inhale and draw the energy up through our right hand and into our heart. We continue breathing in and out, sending the energy down and around as we exhale, drawing it up and into our heart as we inhale.

I ask people to feel and visualize the energy moving around the circle, connecting us all in a circle of love, joy and protection. *Breathe in and draw the energy up, exhale and send the energy down and around.* And, even if you're alone in your circle, it works in awakening you to the exchange of energies because each breath connects you to the plants. The experience is always profound.

I always check in with the participants at this point because someone may feel a bit nauseous or dizzy. They simply need to ground – hands and feet on the ground, no roots, just let the excess energies drain back into Mother Earth. Eating something without sugar and drinking water also helps, as does normal breathing.

When they feel better *physically*, move on to Honor the Directions (step 7). There's always a delicate balance between attending to the needs of one person and the needs of everyone else, so if s/he doesn't improve within a few minutes, ask her/him to sit outside the circle until s/he feels better and continue with the next steps.

The experience can also leave someone feeling vulnerable or angry and they might project that onto you later, so be patient and compassionate. But remember, and remind them, circles are always safe and sacred spaces and there's nothing to fear or worry about.

7. Honor the Directions

The next step is also called Invoking or Welcoming the Directions or Elements, or old style, Summoning the Guardians of the Watchtowers and Opening the Portals for the Elementals, a remnant of ceremonial language.

Honoring the Four Directions is a common part of Indigenous traditions, which also honor Father Sun above, Mother Earth below and the Center, the Source of Creation. (The Native American Medicine Wheel is an example.) The practice is a kind of active meditation that moves us around the compass rose, guiding our spirits through the world in which we live and the inner journeys we take.

The old model inherited from ceremonial traditions was to summon and command the elemental spirits of each direction to appear and do the magician's bidding. My approach is different. I invite, honor and express my respect and gratitude to the Nature beings, the elements and their spirits for their presence and blessings in my life, my circle and the world in which I live.

And as we address the directions, we experience how the boundary between inner and outer is permeable, how we are One with all of Creation. Read the greeting invocations. With repetition, and understanding of the meaning, you'll find yourself naturally memorizing them. Then feel free to write your own, and finally, speak from your heart. You'll be amazed and inspired by the beauty, eloquence and divine wisdom that is within you,

Physically, the old style was to stand in the direction, facing outward, and open a portal for the elementals to enter the circle by drawing an 'invoking pentagram' in the air – the way you'd draw a five-pointed star on paper. We'd visualize a flaming star of the corresponding color and summon the elementals to appear. I prefer to simply reach my arms outward, opening my heart and so opening the circle as I invite the elemental and Nature spirits to join me.

For the East and Air and the South and the Sun/Fire, my arms are upward; for West I raise one hand to the sky for rain and extend the other down toward the oceans, rivers, streams; and for North I hold my palms toward Mother Earth, sometimes kneeling to touch her.

If you're in the Northern Hemisphere, you begin in the East, then move to the South, West and North. In the Southern Hemisphere, start in the East, then North, West and South. *Deosil*. Take your time, feel the energies of each direction, the elemental spirits arriving in the circle, touching you and blessing you. Feel how what is part of the world is part of you.

Move *deosil* around the circle to the next direction until you've returned to the East. Acknowledge the East by raising your arms, then return to your altar and reach up to honor the Father Sun, down to honor Mother Earth, and to the altar to honor the Center, Spirit, source of Creation. The four Invocations of the Elements (Honoring the Four Directions) are on pages 88–90.

Finish by saying: *'My (our) circle is cast, I am (we are) between the worlds.'* You may also wish to use this lovely old chant: *'Air I am, Fire I am, Water, Earth and Spirit I am.'*

8. Honor/Invoke the Sacred/Goddess/God

In traditional Wiccan circles, the Priestess would often Draw Down the Goddess to invoke Her presence in the circle. And sometimes, the Priest would Draw Down the God. Now, women Draw Down the God, and men the Goddess and there's more exploration beyond traditional gender identity.

Drawing Down is a powerful practice that takes time to master, but there are many ways to experience the vital presence of the Goddess, God and the divinity beyond gender. We've already explored several of these in the preceding chapters and we'll explore several more in the chapters devoted to the Goddess and God. A simple invitation from your heart is all you need to offer.

9. State the purpose or intent of the circle

This can also be done before honoring/invoking the Sacred.

10. Make magic

Working with/running/moving divine energy:

Grail

Open yourself to receive divine energy to charge your intention and magic. We've begun to explore this with meditation, breathing and grounding – practices that we'll explore further in upcoming chapters.

Wand

Raise energy from within and the Earth to manifest your intention and magic. We've explored this with chanting and grounding, practices that we'll explore further in upcoming chapters.

11. Offer libation and share cakes/bread

When your magic is done, offer a libation – the ancient practice of pouring a liquid like wine or juice as a religious offering. It's one of my favorite moments, when each person shares the wisdom they've received, and it's always deeply moving.

As always, grace is found in simplicity. When you set up your altar, pour some wine or juice into the chalice (cup) or bowl of the Goddess and place bread or cakes beneath the altar. The Goddess's chalice is passed, _deosil_, around the circle and each person offers his or her libation. When it's time to offer yours, hold the chalice and your cup and speak from your heart, expressing what you've learned from your communion with the Sacred. You may wish to write this in your magical journal.

Then pour some wine or juice from your cup/chalice into the Goddess's and take a drink from your own. If you're working with others, pass the Goddess's chalice to the person to your left, who will do as you did, and then pass the chalice on. If you prefer, you can remain silent.

Once everyone has shared their libation, sprinkle some of the wine or juice onto the bread. The traditional blessing is: *'Bless this bread unto our bodies, bestowing the gifts of health, wealth, joy and the eternal blessing which is love.'*

Break off a piece of the bread, put it in the Goddess's cup, have a bite and pass the bread around the circle to share. It's time to relax and 'feast,' which is also grounding and replenishing of your energy. When you're done, leave an offering for the birds and animals, even if it's crumbs on your windowsill, and pour the rest of the libation on the ground, if possible, or into running water.

12–14. Give thanks and open/close circle

It's important to end circle properly and to release and disperse the energies that have been generated. I've heard endless stories from people about their computers crashing because they forgot to close.

When you're ready to close, thank the Sacred, Goddess, God for being with you and blessing you. Beginning in the East, reach out and thank the elemental and Nature spirits for being with you and blessing you. You can read the invocations but instead of calling and inviting them to circle, *thank them for being present in the circle and with you*. Conclude with the old phrase *'Hail and farewell!'*

Move *widdershins*, counter-Sunwise, around the circle, stopping in each direction to express your gratitude and say farewell, until you return to the East. Finally, turn toward the altar and say: *'Circle is open but never broken.'* (This phrase may be why we use open and close interchangeably when referring to the end of circle.) And if you're with others, add the traditional: *'Merry meet and merry part and merry meet again!'* Hugs and kisses all round.

15. Put away your altar

Clean up the space and return everything to as it was before circle was cast.

More advice for circle etiquette

Cutting out

If you need to leave the circle, simply face outward and cut an arched doorway by moving your hand from left to right at just above head height. Step through and close it behind you by moving your hand across the 'opening.' When you want to re-enter, simply cut another archway, this time from right to left, step through and again, close it behind you. It's important to do this, so don't forget.

Moving within the circle

Food and drink, or materials you're working with to make your magic, or people moving within the circle are all done *deosil*, unless the magic itself calls for moving *widdershins*; but once performed, the rest of the movement within the circle will be *deosil*.

Quiet please

People are often energized in circle and can become very chatty; however, it's important to pay attention to the guidance of the Priestess or whomever is directing the circle's work, to the flow of energies shared by everyone, and to others when they are speaking, especially during libations. In other words, be polite, be respectful and focus.

Circle of Protection

The reality of a circle's boundary has another ancient use: protection. It's a remnant from the old ceremonial traditions that the circle is not just a container to keep magical energies *in* but a protective barrier to keep negative energies *out*. I don't emphasize the need for protection against hostile or disruptive energies, *but* there are times when a circle can be a useful barrier to surround and protect you should you need it.

Just visualize and send out a sphere of protective light from the center of your belly, your power center. Visualize and feel the sphere of light surrounding you. Think of Glinda, the Good Witch of the North, traveling about in her bubble of sparkling energy. That may sound silly, but protective spheres are powerful and effective when you need them.

At the center of the circle

Casting circle, fully present in each cardinal communion, is a journey to balance and wholeness. Each step is an encounter with your own holiness shared with the holiness of the world that encircles you. Cast circle and you welcome divinity into the world, discover the magic between the worlds and make the magic that can change the world, and *you*. Cast circle and *you* are at its Center, where Spirit enters Creation. *You* are the magic the universe makes.

So let us end where we began, with a lovely chant:

> *'We are a circle within a circle, with no beginning and never ending.'*

Chapter 7

Goddess

'We all come from the Goddess, and to Her we shall return, like a drop of rain, flowing to the ocean...'

The chant evaporates. I reach up to seize the waning Moon's sharp curve, to command its gleaning power in this wise time in my life. I hear the voices of others singing with me, but I stand alone, in my garden, within the circle I have cast. Holding the sickle, I feel Her presence, energizing and encircling me, moving with me as I begin to sway, to dance, to harvest my dreams...

The first time I saw the Goddess was in my dreams, but the first time I recognized Her in the world was in my first circle. She was singing, dancing and laughing, Her light shining in the eyes of the women beside me. She was embodied in their energies, personalities and passions: Artemis in the strength of one, Pele in the sensual fire of another, Rhea in the maternal power of the Priestess.

I began to realize that if the Goddess lived in them, perhaps She also lived in me.

You don't *believe* in the Goddess. You *experience* Her. She is embodied by all women, and resides within all of us, regardless of our gender. She is equally important to men, and to all those challenging the damaging constraints of patriarchy, regardless of gender identification, because She restores balance and wholeness.

She is the infinite Source of Creation, embodied by Creation in its infinite diversity. She has been with us since the beginning of human awakening and hidden from us for thousands of years by suppression. Blind to Her wisdom and Her ways, humanity has created a world dangerously out of balance. But the Great Goddess, the missing half of everything, has returned.

Practice: Goddess blessing

Stand before a mirror, cross your arms over your chest, look into your eyes, and recite the following:

> 'Great Goddess who dwells within and all around me,
> Goddess of the shining Moon and the fertile Earth,
> Goddess of the starry heavens and womb of Creation,
> Goddess from whom all blessings flow,
> Bless your child.'

Close your eyes, breathe and feel your heart open. Invite the Goddess to be with you and rest in the love you feel. Open your eyes and see the light of the Goddess shining in you. When you're done, close your arms, give yourself a hug and give Her thanks. Write about your experience in your magical journal.

The Charge of the Goddess

The Goddess is the mirror in which we find the lost and sacred parts of ourselves, and of the world in which we live. She is more than a symbol or inner archetype. The Great Goddess is the ground of being and the Mystery beyond knowing, Creation and the Source of Creation. Our relationship with Her is vital to the fulfillment of our lives and the future of life on Earth.

There are many ways to welcome Her presence within our hearts and in the world. One of the most beautiful Goddess invocations is *The Charge of the Goddess*, which is read or recited in circles all over the world and used to Draw Down the Goddess – a trance technique in which the Goddess enters the invoker to see, speak and bless those who are present.

The Charge of the Goddess was written many years ago by Doreen Valiente. Below is her latest version, which her Foundation graciously granted permission to be reproduced here as her 'best copy' and thus most 'official.' Woven from many sources, its language is archaic but it's beauty, wisdom and power are ageless, and its impact on the speaker and the listener magical:

The Charge of the Goddess

Listen to the words of the Great Mother, who was of old also called Artemis; Astarte; Diana; Melusine; Aphrodite; Cerridwen; Dana; Arianrhod; Isis; Bride; and by many other names.

Whenever ye have need of anything, once in a month, and better it be when the Moon be full, then ye shall assemble in some secret place and adore the spirit of me, who am Queen of all Witcheries.

There shall ye assemble, ye who are fain to learn all sorcery, yet have not yet won its deepest secrets: to these will I teach things that are yet unknown.

And ye shall be free from slavery; and as a sign that ye are really free, ye shall be naked in your rites; and ye shall dance, sing, feast, make music and love, all in my praise.

For mine is the ecstasy of the spirit and mine also is joy on earth; for my Law is Love unto all Beings.

Keep pure your highest ideal; strive ever toward it; let naught stop you or turn you aside.

For mine is the secret door which opens upon the Land of Youth; and mine is the Cup of the Wine of Life, and the Cauldron of Cerridwen, which is the Holy Grail of Immortality.

I am the Gracious Goddess, who gives the gift of joy unto the heart. Upon earth, I give the knowledge of the spirit eternal; and beyond death, I give peace, and freedom, and reunion with those who have gone before. Nor do I demand sacrifice, for behold I am the Mother of All Living, and my love is poured out upon the earth.

Hear ye the words of the Star Goddess, she in the dust of whose feet are the hosts of heaven; whose body encircleth the universe; I, who am the beauty of the green Earth, and the white Moon among the stars, and the mystery of the waters, and the heart's desire, call unto thy soul. Arise and come unto me.

For I am the Soul of Nature, who giveth life to the universe; from me all things proceed, and unto me must all things return; and before my face, beloved of gods and mortals, thine inmost divine self shall be unfolded in the rapture of infinite joy.

Let my worship be within the heart that rejoiceth, for behold: all acts of love and pleasure are my rituals. And therefore let there be beauty and strength, power and compassion, honour and humility, mirth and reverence within you.

And thou who thinkest to seek for me, know thy seeking and yearning shall avail thee not, unless thou know this Mystery: that if that which thou seekest thou findest not within thee, thou wilt never find it without thee.

For behold, I have been with thee from the beginning; and I am that which is attained at the end of desire.

Mother Earth

We're all born and live in the lap of the Goddess. Regardless of our religion, culture, race or gender, we're all children of Mother Earth. How old were you the first time you heard the expression Mother Earth? On some level we all know it's true. Like other Indigenous peoples, our ancestors revered Her. Some of the earliest human depictions of the Divine are pictographs and symbols of the Feminine and female figurines dating back to 28,000BCE.

Great Mother, Gaia, Demeter, Terra Mater, Cels, Nerthus, Danu, Brigantia, Frigga and so many more, Her rites were the foundation of our first civilizations. Say them aloud and the Earth stirs to reawakening, responding to the calls of Her children. Say them aloud and *you're* re-awakening, responding to Her calls to us. At this moment of environmental crisis, when the future of life on Earth is imperiled, She *is* calling us.

Just as She nourishes our body, She nourishes our spirit and everything we need to know to transform death into rebirth, to live rich in body and soul, to rediscover our purpose and experience the love of Creation, is right in front of us. We just need to pay attention and pay respect.

Practice: Mother Earth's heartbeat

Take an offering, such as birdseed, a receipt from a donation to an environmental organization or a commitment for Her care you are going to make, and your magical journal and head outside to your place of power or a spot that calls to you.

❖ Sit on the Earth. Breathe and ground. Take your time. Feel the energy of Mother Earth filling and nourishing you. Place your hand on the breast of Mother Earth. Feel the ground beneath you, the warmth, the energy.

❖ With your hand, gently tap the rhythm of your heartbeat: *bum bump pause bum bump pause...* Feel your heart's rhythm in harmony with Mother Earth's heart. Feel Her strength beneath you, Her energies flowing through you, Her love filling you. Think of all of Her countless, generous blessings to you and how She nourishes and sustains your body *and* soul. Thank Her. Listen to the sounds of Mother Earth – the birds, the leaves of the trees rustling, Her other children who share Her blessings with you. How do you feel?

❖ Write about your experience in your magical journal. Reflect on how to give back, to give thanks to Mother Earth. Make your offering. Next time, you may also wish to do this using a drum. Pay attention to how you treat Mother Earth every day, and remember to give thanks and reciprocate Her blessings.

The Goddess's countless names

The Goddess is One and many, the Great Mother and more than a mother. She is the Great Goddess and the myriad

Goddesses revered across the globe and throughout human history. Goddesses are makers of magic and civilization, warriors and bestowers of peace, protectors of animals and hunters; they are unconquerably sexual, and crones with more important matters to attend to; they are ecstatic and compassionate, the source of Creation and destruction.

Goddesses restore our esteem for the feminine and at the same time challenge the old ideas about gender, about what is feminine and what is masculine. The Goddess moves our thinking beyond dualities and the limitations of either/or. She reminds us to embrace both/and, often embodying opposing qualities. And while often envisioned in human form, She is natural energy beyond anthropomorphic appearance. Some Goddesses are part animal, like the lion-headed Goddess Sekhmet; some are forces of Nature, like Oya, the great storm, revealing Nature's divine power and order; some are the Mystery beyond human knowing.

Practice: Goddess chant

'Isis, Astarte, Diana, Hecate, Demeter, Kali, Inanna.'

Repeat this chant by Deena Metzger again and again. Dance as you chant, until you feel your heart open; until you feel Her dancing with you.

Seek Her and you will see Her. Call Her and She will come: *Spiderwoman, Shekina, Yemaya, Maat, Mary, Kuan Yin, Kali, Demeter, Minerva, Freyja...* and so many more. Chanting Her/their names always feels like I'm participating in the magic of Her/their rebirth, and my own. The more you come to know them, the more you'll come to know yourself.

A short list of Goddesses

Creation
Tefnut (Egyptian), Shakti (Hindu), Ishtar (Babylonian), Amaterasu (Japanese Shinto), Al-Lat (Arabian), Nu Kua (Chinese), Tara (Buddhist)

Earth, prosperity, fertility
Gaia, Demeter (Greek), Ceres (Roman), Fortuna (Etruscan), Freyja (Norse), Sovereignty (Celtic), Brigantia (British), Lakshmi (Hindu), Mokosh (Slavic), Mami Wata (African), Mazu (Chinese)

Magic and transformation
Isis (Egyptian), Hecate (Greek), Cerridwen (Celtic), Tana (Estrucan), Thorgerd (Icelandic), Freyja (Norse), Loviatar (Finnish, Sami)

Guides through darkness
Isis (Egyptian), Hecate, Persephone (Greek), Inanna (Sumerian)

Love
Aphrodite (Greek), Venus (Roman), Bronwyn (Welsh), Freyja (Norse), Oshun (Yoruban, Voudou), Shakti (Hindu)

Culture, art, wisdom

Athena (Greek), Minerva (Roman), Hokmah (Hebrew), Brigid (Celtic), Spiderwoman (Native American), Princess Liêu Hanh (Taoist)

Healing and rebirth

Cerridwen, Brigid (Celtic), Isis (Egyptian), Hera (Greek), Diana (Roman), Kuan Yin, Tara (Buddhist)

Warriors

Morrigan (Celtic), Amaterasu (Japanese Shinto), Kali, Durga (Hindu), Athena, Artemis (Greek), Sekhmet (Egyptian), Bellona (Roman), Ixchel (Mayan), Hel (Norse)

Justice

Maat, Sekhmet (Egyptian), Themis, Hecate (Greek), Oya (Yoruban, Voudou), Kali (Hindu), Hel (Norse)

The Goddess who guides you

There are countless Goddesses, each with Her own blessings and gifts, powers and purposes, symbols and stories, totem animals and magical plants, invocations, energies, manifestations and Mysteries. There's a particular Goddess who calls to each of us. When we open our hearts to Her, She will guide us. She will challenge and transform, nourish and empower us to become whole, to become sacred, to become who we're meant to be.

How do you find Her? Certainly you can read, research and reflect. When I began my journey, there were very few books about Goddesses, or the Divine Feminine. Now there are countless resources and this chapter, I hope, will help you. But before you immerse yourself in books, invite the Goddess to come to you by *Her* ways of knowing – dreaming and intuition, following your sixth sense and the signs She sends you.

Use a Goddess Tarot deck and pull a card revealing Her name or let a book of Goddesses fall open to Her description. Listen for Her voice in poetry and meditation and in the stirrings of something sacred within you. Honor your desire to encounter Her and trust your ability to open yourself and offer your heart, like the Holy Grail, to receive Her. She will find *you*.

Guided visualization: Meet the Goddess

This is an adaptation of the Storytelling guided visualization (*see page 52*); you can record and listen to this, or read it. Follow the wording of Storytelling until you reach **Exhale and return it**; then continue with the text below.

A small, beautiful owl appears suddenly, flying silently over your head. It circles above you and then flies off, then circles back to you, and flies off as you follow it through the magical meadow you've visited before.

In the distance is the stand of trees and you feel your heart race with excitement as you enter the cool forest. The owl leads you past the stream you've visited before. You walk deeper into the woods, where the light grows soft and green, the Sun hidden by the canopy of thick leaves and interwoven branches high above.

The owl disappears, and just as you worry that you're alone in this dark wood, there is a wild and swirling rush of air as owl lands on your shoulder. You can feel its talons scrape your skin, and it thrills you to have this creature so close, to feel its power and sense its otherworldly wisdom. You look into owl's enormous, blinking eyes, see the complex pattern of its feathers and recognize that you're in the presence of magic.

The owl speaks: *'Before you is the sacred grove of the Goddess. Only those who come with perfect love and perfect trust may enter.'* It explodes into flight, the power of its wings thrusting you forward into the circle of guardian oaks that has appeared before you.

In the center of the clearing stands a woman, her back to you. Her voice fills the tree-ringed circle as she asks: *'What is it you seek?'* She turns and faces you. Is she a young woman, a mother, an elder? She may be dark as night or made of light, ringed with flowers or flames, floating on water or air. She is the Goddess who guides you.

In your hands is an offering. Place it on the ground before Her. Open your heart and tell Her what is there. Speak honestly and don't fear Her judgment. Ask Her for what you need. Listen carefully to what She says. She reaches out and touches your heart.

Close your eyes. Feel the energy of Her blessing flow into you. Feel your heart open. Feel your heart healing, your body healing. Feel your spirit heal. Feel Her energy coursing through you, renewing you, strengthening you, giving you all that you need – vision, confidence, love, fulfillment. Feel Her blessing you, feel Her Love for you. Rest in Her blessing, Her love.

Open your eyes. You're alone in the sacred grove. She has taken your offering and left you with Her name and the knowledge that She watches over you. Turn and take the path back through the forest, through the meadow, where the Sun has now dropped to the horizon. Turn around. The Sun has set and the Moon is rising. The meadow disappears into night.

It's time to return. Feel your body. Stretch your fingers, toes, arms and legs. When you're ready, open your eyes. In your magical journal, write about your encounter, what you discovered and how you feel.

Once you've met your Goddess, create an altar to Her using her symbols and objects that represent Her gifts and powers.

**Make room for the Goddess in your life
and you make room for yourself.**

Practice: Creating an altar and offerings for your Goddess

The altar

Use the colors, flowers, plants, herbs, fruits and elements that are associated with Her. Create or find an image of Her for the altar. Create a potion or incense using herbs that are special to Her, or a bouquet with Her flowers and herbs; prepare a dish using foods, fruits and vegetables that are sacred to Her.

The offerings

Create a gift of gratitude for the Goddess that expresses your creativity and reflects some aspect of Her meaning or blessings for you.

Write or create a work of art or performance, cook or plant something, sew or do any kind of craft – whatever expresses the best about you. Don't judge it as anything except beautiful, heartfelt and appreciated.

The altar is going to be more beautiful than you could possibly imagine. You've embodied Her spirit and yours – spend some time enjoying the beauty you've created.

The Triple Goddess and the Moon

The Moon governs the Earth's tides and growing cycles. Though there are also Gods of the Moon, the Moon remains one of the most ancient and potent symbols of the Goddess: Diana, Luna, Artemis, Selene, Ishtar, Neith, Yemaya, Arianrhod, Heng O, Raka, Mama Killa and Hecate – who was frequently depicted in Threefold form, the Triple Goddess of Maiden, Mother and Crone – even Mary, who borrowed the crescent crown from Isis.

For everyone, everywhere, the Moon is a mirror *and* a portal into the cyclical realm of our inner Divine Feminine, the subconscious, intuition and deepest feelings, the spiritual powers deep within us all. But the Divine Moon is more than a symbol – She is the Goddess who shares the rhythmic, embodied wisdom of women.

After millennia of domination, restriction and taboo, women are rediscovering and reclaiming their innate spiritual power, their Mysteries. Many of these are blood Mysteries – the connection between the Moon's monthly

28-day cycle and women's menstrual cycles, and the connection between the Goddess as Maiden, Mother and Crone and the stages of women's lives. *The lunar blood Mysteries remind women that our bodies are sacred.*

It's impossible to explain the profound change in perception, the freedom and empowerment that comes when 'the curse' lifts and the life force is revealed. A religious revolution is under way as women reclaim the sacred wisdom and life-giving power of their bodies, recreating rites and ceremonies of self-definition, empowerment and spiritual awakening. The Moon reminds everyone that spiritual wisdom and power are *embodied*, by the Earth and by each of us.

Behind the Moon – beyond gender

Of course, not all women bleed, not all women give birth to children, not all women wish to be defined as women because of their body. There are great transformations and challenges being raised today about gender and self-identification.

The sisterhood of women has boundaries that are increasingly permeable, a dynamic as ancient as the Priests of Cybele who practiced self-castration, shamanic traditions of double or twin souls, and Indigenous initiations of young men that involved cutting a wound in their upper thighs that bled. These are different holy Mysteries, a different path to the Goddess, with their own wisdom, power and magic.

And there are many places where paths intertwine, where circles overlap or move within larger circles. There's the path of men, for those who identify as gender non-specific or gender-fluid, for whom the Goddess, lunar and in all other forms, is a vital part of their spiritual journey and wholeness. She restores lost parts of all of us, provides healing to our psyches and souls wounded by patriarchy.

What is most important is that we support and respect each other's revelations and Mysteries. Regardless of gender, the lunar Goddesses also offer blessings to us all, which we can share and rejoice in together. And among these blessings is the magic of transformation, growth and manifestation.

Practice: Invoking your Goddess

Below is a simple, but powerful way to invoke your Goddess, whether lunar or other.

1. Create your Goddess altar.

2. Cast your circle.

3. Place your offering on the altar.

4. Invoke your Goddess. Do this as follows:

   ❖ Write your invocation beforehand or simply speak from your heart.

   ❖ Explain your offering and how She has spoken to your needs and longings.

✦   Ask for Her guidance, ask to be shown how to integrate Her powers into your life, how to receive Her blessings and how to reciprocate.

5. Meditate and visualize Her inspiration transforming your life. Feel Her presence within you and all around you. Reflect, chant, dance, allow Her to move within you and through you. Thank Her for the blessings She's giving you.

6. Close your circle. You may wish to keep the altar up as a focal point for daily meditations, offerings and magical work with your Goddess, the Moon and your/Her Mysteries.

Devote a journal to your Goddess work. In it, write about the wisdom, power and gifts of the Goddess and how you'll integrate them into your life.

Moon magic

The phases of the Moon often determine what kind of spiritual and magical work you will do. Below I've adapted a profound traditional practice, Drawing Down the Moon, which you can tailor to work with each of the three phases of the Moon and aspects of the Triple Goddess – waxing/Maiden, full/Mother and waning/ Crone – using the Wisdom of the Moon I've provided here.

The wisdom of the Moon

Maiden

Moon phase: New/waxing.

Maiden Goddesses: Artemis, Kore, Athena, Diana, Luna, Nimue, Sekhmet, Morrigan, Lady of the Wild Things.

Qualities: Free; independent; virginal (meaning a woman unto herself); wild; active; awakening to power; youthful; a hunter and protector of wild animals; a warrior.

Magic: New projects; preparing for battle; finding your strength; honoring your instincts; finding your freedom and your courage.

Color: White.

Invocation: *'I call upon the powers of the mighty Goddess (Diana), power of the new Moon, Lady of the Wild Things. Strengthen and free me to live the life I want. Charge and bless me.'*

Chant: *'Lady of the Wild Things, free me, strengthen me.'*

Mother

Moon phase: Full.

Mother Goddesses: Isis, Hathor, Semele, Cybele, Gaia, Demeter, Ceres, Yemaya, Shakti, Pachamama, Rhiannon, Freyja, Divine Mother, Great Mother.

Qualities: Loving and compassionate; powerful; source of Creation and creativity; sexual; fertile; fruitful; nurturing; generous.

Magic: Making things grow and manifest; bestowing blessings on others; healing; creating wholeness; honoring creative projects.

Color: Red.

Invocation: *'Great Goddess of the Glorious Mother Moon, I invoke you. Shine your light upon me. Bless me with your radiant power to make my dreams come true. Bless me with abundance.'*

Chant: *'One thing becomes another, in the Mother, in the Mother.'*

Crone

Moon phase: Waning or dark.

Crone Goddesses: Cerridwen, Lusaaset, Hecate (modern conception), Baba Yaga, Grandmother Spiderwoman, Chthonia, Wise One, Tefnut, Hel.

Qualities: Wisdom; magic; banishing; choices; death; challenger and guide through dark times and underworlds.

Magic: Prophecy; truth-telling; transformation; transitions; endings; banishing; death; justice; shamanism; movement between worlds.

Color: Black.

Invocation: *'Goddess of the magic at the crossroads, I invoke you: You walk in all the realms, help me let go of what holds me back, guide me through the darkness, through the light. Bless me with your wisdom.'*

Chant: *'She changes everything She touches and everything She touches changes.'*

It's deeply empowering for women to discover that each aspect of the Triple Goddess contains the preceding one within Her – so Mother is also Maiden and Crone is also Mother and Maiden – don't forget to honor them all in your work and your life.

Practice: Drawing Down the Moon

Drawing Down is a powerful trance technique that's traditionally performed by the Priestess to enlighten and bless. Below is another way of Drawing Down that's accessible and still powerful if you're just beginning to encounter the Goddess.

1. First, reflect on where you are in your life, your spiritual journey. Reflect on which aspect of the Triple Goddess can best assist you. Pay attention to the phases of the Moon and when the moment arrives, go outside and stand beneath it, if you can. At least try to see it from your window.

2. Cast a circle around yourself.

3. Recite the Goddess Blessing or read *The Charge of the Goddess* (both above).

4. Cross your arms over your chest and gaze into the Moon, Diana's Mirror; the new Moon inspiring us to hope, the manifesting mirror of the Divine Mother, the Crone's sickle ready to cut away the outworn from your life. Breathe and let the feeling of Her presence come to you, from within and without.

5. Close your eyes if you wish. When you feel the energy beginning to flow, filling and overflowing the chalice of your heart, uncross your arms, and with your elbows still bent and palms facing

outward, even with your shoulders – the Goddess position – feel Her presence for as long as She is with you. When you feel the energies receding, close your arms.

6. Wrap yourself in a warm blanket and pour a libation for Her. Eat and drink something to ground yourself. Write about your experience in your magical journal. Get a good night's rest.

Blessings of the Goddess

We're standing at a crossroad in history, a moment when we must choose what our future will be. There's a Goddess at this crossroad – ancient, wise, full of terror and challenge, magic and justice. If we have the courage to face Her, to risk being confronted with the truth of who we have been, She will guide us through the darkness of ignorance, greed and domination.

She will dismember our lifeless institutions, values and assumptions, and guide us safely through the barren landscape of death, revealing the holy magic of the cosmos and blessing us with rebirth. She will guide us to who we're meant to be and why we're here. When you are ready, call Her.

Chapter 8

God

It's been a dark and snow-covered winter, but today the Sun is stronger and warmer on skin and Earth. The snows have melted and the ground has opened to emerging magic. A pale green spear, God has returned to the world. I stand on ground that is giving birth to hope.

The God that Wicca has rediscovered does not dwell alone in a distant Heaven. He's One and many, in the world and in us. And this God is always, in some form or another, the Goddess's partner. Together, they embody love.

The relationship of Goddess and God, the Divine Couple, is the mytho-poetry of the Wiccan holy calendar. Their annual dance is the eternal, seasonal, life-engendering cycle of Earth and Sun. Together they unify polarities and all points between, and their union encircles all within and beyond traditional gender definition. We'll explore their relationship and discover more about the God as a loving partner in Chapter 9, The Wheel of the Year.

Rediscovering God

Like the Goddess, rediscovering a God who is present, joyful and a loving partner transforms *ideas* about divinity into *experiences* of divinity, and that changes our humanity. The God restores and heals what's been missing in men *and* women and in the world. He's playful, sensual and emotional. This God is embodied and waiting to be encountered.

The place to discover Him is not in books or ideas. You'll find him in the Other World, but the most important encounters will be where you rarely look – within yourself and in the natural world. He's most accessible when you're fully present in the pursuits about which you're passionate – pay attention to what you love and the God will be present.

The God embodies an entirely new masculinity for men and has a profound impact on women. He is the opposite of the patriarchal God, freeing men and empowering women to be all that the culture and its religions have long denied them. Open your heart, invite Him into your life and He will appear.

Practice: God Spell

Each day for the next week, stand before a mirror, arms crossed over your chest in the God position, look into your own eyes and recite the following spell (memorize or record it as you look into the mirror):

'Great God who dwells within and all around me, God from whom the breath of life and inspiration comes, God of the shining Sun and the cleansing seas, God of the wild things and the seeds of new life within me, God of love and rejoicing, be reborn within me!'

As you finish, close your eyes and feel His presence rising within you. Feel the energy, the vitality and joy coursing through you, healing your heart, filling all the empty spaces with love and power.

When you're ready, open your eyes and see the light of the God shining from you. When the energy peaks, close your eyes and give thanks. Feel the energy ebb and when you're ready, open your eyes. Smile. Write about your experience in your magical journal.

The God who guides you

As we discover the God within ourselves, we tap into a powerful source of energy, creativity and self-confidence. The God within is the God who guides you at this moment in your life. He appears in countless aspects and manifestations and offers many paths and sources of wisdom, empowerment and growth as you come into the fullness of your embodied spirit. There's a God who calls to you, who watches over and guides you, and He will materialize in whatever shape you need to come into balance and fulfillment.

A short list of Gods

As with many Goddesses, Gods embody more than one quality, often joining opposing aspects. These Gods are often personifications of natural energies, forces of Nature with human traits. This is a very select list to begin your discovery of the God(s) and to inspire you to delve deeper.

Creation

Zeus (Greek), Jupiter (Roman), Shango (Yoruban, Voudou), Rainbow Serpent (Aboriginal Australian), Amun (Egyptian), Pacha Kamaq (Incan), El (Canaanite, Hebrew)

Nature, fertility

Plants: Dionysus as Vine, Adonis (Greek), Osiris (Egyptian), Tammuz (Sumerian), Dumuzi (Mesopotamian), Mescalito (Native American), Oshosi (Yoruban, Voudou), Jack-in-the Green, Green Man (British, Celtic), Fufluns (Etruscan)

Animals (Horned Gods)

Dionysus as Bull, Pan (Greek), Cernunnos (Celtic), Herne (British), Apis (Egyptian), Aja (Yoruban)

Magic, transformation

Gwyddien (Welsh), Shango (Yoruban, Voudou), Veles (Slavic), Thoth (Egyptian), Hermes (Greek), Bluetongue Lizard (Aboriginal Australian), Odin (Norse)

Love and sexuality

Eros (Greek), Aengus (Celtic), Mabon (Welsh), Hermaphroditus (Greek, gender fluid), Xochipilli (Aztec), Min (Egyptian)

Culture, wisdom

Mimir, Odin (Norse), Ogma (Celtic), Chokmah (Hebrew), Ganesha, Brahma (Hindu), Apollo, Hermes (Greek), Thoth (Egyptian), Orunmila (Yoruba, Latin American), Lao Zi (Chinese), Enki (Mesopotamian)

Trickster

Loki (Norse), Coyote (Native American), Crow (Aboriginal Australian), Set (Egyptian)

Healing

Apollo, Asclepius, Chiron (Greek), Agwu (African), Ixtlilton (Aztec), Dian Cecht (Irish), Hua Tuo (Chinese), Dhanvantari (Hindu), Erinle (Yoruban, Voudou)

Warrior

Ares (Greek), Mars (Roman), Ogun (Yoruban, Voudou), Mixcoatl (Aztec), Cicolluis (Irish, Gaulish), Teutates (British, Gaulish), Anhur (Egyptian), Mangala (Hindu), Dayisun Tngri (Mongolian shamanism), Odin, Thor, Ullr (Norse)

Justice

Odin, Forseti, Tyr (Norse), Zeus (Greek), Jupiter (Roman), Shango (Yoruban, Voudou), Rod (Slavic), Enlil (Sumerian), Shiva (Hindu), Haukim (pre-Islamic Arabian), Issitoq (Inuit)

Below is a guided visualization you can use to encounter the God who guides you. And as with the Goddess, you can also journey to meet Him.

Guided visualization: Find the God within

This is an adaptation of the Storytelling guided visualization (*see page 52*); you can record and listen to this, or read it. Follow the wording of Storytelling, until you reach **Exhale and return it**; then continue with the text below.

A broad-chested, great antlered stag stands before you. It circles around you and then takes off running; it circles back to you, and runs off again. You follow it though the meadow you visited before. You see the stand of trees at the end of the meadow and once again you feel your heart race with excitement. You enter the woods and the stag leads you past the stream. You walk deeper into the woods, where the Sun is hidden by the canopy above.

The stag disappears, and just as you worry that you're alone in this dark wood, it reappears behind you. You can feel its breath on your skin and it thrills you to have this magical creature standing so close, to feel its power and sense its otherworldly wisdom. You look into its dark eyes and recognize that you're in the presence of magic.

The stag speaks: *'Before you is the sacred grove of the God. Only those who come with perfect love and perfect trust may enter.'* It then pivots and runs off, the power of its movement propelling you into the circle of guardian oaks that opens before you.

Within the circle of towering trees is a circle of ancient standing stones, towering over you. In the center, a man, tall and broad-shouldered, stands with his back to you. Without turning, He asks you: *'What is it you seek?'* You look up into the Sun, high in the sky above the trees, the stones, the two of you. Momentarily blinded by the Sun's brilliance, you close your eyes and when you open them, He's facing you.

Is He old? Is He young? Does He wear an antlered crown? Or is there a halo made by the Sun surrounding His head? Is He covered with leaves? Does He carry pipes or a sword, a hammer or a book? Is there an animal by His side?

Answer Him. Tell him what's in your heart. Speak honestly and don't fear his judgment. Ask the questions you need to, share the feeling you want to. Listen carefully as He responds to what you've said.

He opens His arms to you and you step into them. Feel them holding you with love, kindness and healing power. Receive the blessing He offers. Let it flow into you. Let your heart open, your wounds be healed, your belly know its fire. Feel the energy, the power and new life flowing through you. Feel your courage, your confidence and your vitality return.

Open your eyes. You are alone. Express your gratitude, leave your offering and return from the stone circle, from the sacred grove, from the woods, through the meadow to your place of beginning. Feel your body. Feel its strength and vitality. Stretch, and when you're ready, open your eyes.

In your magical journal, write about who you encountered, what you asked him, what he said, what you discovered and how you feel.

Just as you did with the Goddess, seek the God through dreams and visualizations, synchronicities and intuition before reading and research. It's a profound experience to encounter Him first and *then* discover who you encountered. And it's deeply moving, validating ways of knowing beyond the intellectual.

As with the Goddess, there's now a wealth of information about ancestral Gods available to help you discern who appeared. And remember, He may not be ancestral. You may be of Norse descent but a Hindu God has called to you, or you may be of African descent but a Native American deity has responded to you. Working with what you've been shown and what you've learned, create an altar honoring the God within, the God who guides you.

The Sun and Men's Mysteries

Magic manifests in our lives as we come into harmony with the great rhythm of the world in which we live. Our ancestors honored the Sun as the son of the Great Mother and as the partner of the Mother Earth. He is the Norse Baldur, the Roman Sol, the Yoruban Shango, the Greek Helios and Apollo, the Celtic Belenus and Irish Lugh.

Just as the constant cycle of light and dark, the perpetual waxing and waning of the Moon is a mirror for women that also offers wisdom to men and the gender-fluid, the Sun is most intimately reflected in the lives of men, also offering wisdom to women and the gender-fluid.

(And of course, there are lunar deities that are male, and solar deities that are female.)

Just as the Moon's cycle of 28 days and three stages corresponds exactly to Women's Mysteries, menstrual and life cycle, the Sun cycle is reflected in the rhythm of men's physical, psychological and spiritual lives. Men's lives wax as they grow from boyhood to manhood, from dependence to maturity, and wane as they age, decline and die. But the Sun returns each year, just as the Moon returns every month.

One of the greatest blessings we all receive from the God is His 'fire in the belly.' As the Goddess is the belly, the God is the fire within it. This is power we share to create new ideas, forms and life. It's also the fire of desire and sexuality: the hormone testosterone gives everyone their sex drive, muscular strength and sense of optimism and determination, and studies have shown that it's affected by the Sun's daily and seasonal waxing and waning. The God is the fire that burns within you.

Practice: Drawing Down the Sun

As with Drawing Down the Moon for women, this is a spiritual practice designed primarily for men, but it can be performed by anyone, regardless of gender identity. The most powerful times of year to Draw Down are between Winter and Summer Solstice, when the powers of the Sun are growing; and the most powerful time of day is when the Sun is high in the sky, preferably outdoors, in your place of power.

Let's begin.

1. Cast your circle. Stand in the center, arms crossed over your chest – the God position. Breathe and ground. Read or memorize and recite the invocation of the Sun God:

    'By fire and light I invoke you,

    By heat and by energy I invoke you,

    By wisdom and by passion I invoke you

    Mighty Sun in the midday sky

    Light your fires within me

    Illuminate my mind, kindle my passion, hone my will,

    Bless my life with your power.'

2. When you feel the God's presence, reach out and grasp the fire of the Sun. Feel it burning between your palms and bring it into your belly and loins. Feel the Sun's energy empowering you. Experience how good and alive you feel. Envision the work, the creation, the goal you've set. See it manifesting.

3. Chant, drum, dance, stamp your feet and pound your chest. Feel the power move within your body. When the energies wane, fold your arms over your chest and open your eyes. See how everything around you is growing. See the light given off by everything: plants, animals, even rocks and the Earth beneath your feet. The Sun resides within everything.

4. Offer thanks. Write about your experience, your goals and your plans in your magical journal.

As you honor the light within yourself, the energies of enlightenment, creativity and growth flow into your life. Your spirit becomes embodied. It shines and illuminates the path before you and the world around you.

The magic of the Green Man

Years ago, celebrating the harvest of the Autumn Equinox in a field of ripe corn, I swung the sickle and as the cut was made, I heard the God speak: *'The Sun goes into the seed!'* It was a revelation. *Forms change but the energy of life is immortal.* The Sun is the fire that galvanizes the Earth's capacity to bear and nourish life. It's the eternal energy of life encased within.

This cycle of transformation *and* transcendence is at the heart of Wicca and all Indigenous wisdom traditions – the union of light and matter, Spirit and Earth in the endless cycle of Creation. The seed, resting within the womb of the Mother, is always reborn. This is the magic of the Green Man. Attend to Mother Earth and you'll find the Green Man. He is Her son, companion and partner, Her advocate and protector. As the Goddess has a Threefold nature, so does the Green Man – He is Spirit, plant and humanity. He is a man covered in green leaves, vines, flowers and fruits who dies and is reborn. He is tree and forest, corn and grain, vine and fruit, and the healing spirit of peyote and other medicine plants.

As the Moon teaches women about the inherent divinity of their bodies, the Green Man teaches men about the holy rhythm of theirs – lessons he teaches all living beings. He embodies and teaches the cyclical certainty of the life force and our life; and the lives of all animals, including humans, are sustained by Him.

The Green Man's symbols and story are shared by Osiris, Dionysus, Tammuz, Adonis, Quetzalcoatl, Mescalito, Oshosi, Jesus, St. George, Jack-in-the-Green and Jack-in-the Pulpit. His image is carved in churches all over England and Europe, and He reappears in the story of Robin Hood, retold to every new generation in books and movies.

Walk into Nature, forest, field, park or garden and the Green Man will teach you the abundance, generosity and profound spiritual wisdom embodied by Nature. He will guide you through the cycles of your own life and share the energies that bring your dreams into being. He'll teach you how to accept the sharp cut when the harvest is complete, to trust the magic of the Sun within the seed and to rest and dream within the darkness. He *will* bring you back to life again.

Practice: Planting seeds of change

The best time of year to make magic with the Green Man is spring, after the first frost, but you can do this inside as well. Have ready a packet of zinnia or other hardy seeds and a small pot with soil in it.

Let's begin.

Head out into Nature, to your place of power if it has a tree, or to the tree teaching you to ground. Address the tree as the Green Man and ask if you may work with Him. You might say: *'Green Man, power of the forest, of the grain, of all green things that grow from Mother Earth, Green Man who feeds me, feed my spirit, teach me how to grow.'*

Sit with your back against the tree's trunk. Hold the seeds and the soil-filled pot in your lap. Pay attention to what you see, hear, smell and feel. Close your eyes. Ground and center. Feel the power of life that makes all things grow; feel it rising and moving through and empowering you. Feel yourself grow stronger, healthier, more joyful. Realize all the good things you're creating in your life. Direct that energy into the seeds and the soil. Listen to what the Green Man has to teach you.

When you're ready, open your eyes. Observe the vitality glowing all around you. Plant three of the seeds in the soil and 'charge it' by directing your energy, the Green Man's gift of energy, into the potted seeds. Visualize your dreams, goals and aspirations growing.

Thank the Green Man, the tree, the grass beneath you, the plant beings all around you. Feel, hear, see their acknowledgment. Take the potted seeds with you and water them. Tend them every day, visualize your goals manifesting and take action every day to make them happen. If the seeds fail, try again. Write about your experiences in your magical journal.

Just remember, every time you eat a piece of bread, a bowl of grain, a vegetable or fruit, every time you take a breath, you're receiving the gift of life from the Green Man, from all the plant beings. Give back with gratitude and know that you're never alone.

The Horned God

Seventeen thousand years ago, an image was painted upon a cave wall in Lascaux, France. It's a man with the head and antlers of a stag. He is another force of Nature, Lord of the Animals, dancing his inseminating magic within the womb of the Mother Earth. Horned Gods are Gods of animal power, of vitality and sex, instinctual wisdom, wild freedom and the holiness of the body and the Earth.

He is the antlered stag-God Herne the Hunter of ancient Britain and the Celtic Cernunnos. He is Apis, the Egyptian bull and son of the Goddess Isis, Poseidon, the sea bull of the Greeks, Mithras and Neptune of the Romans. He's the goat-foot God Pan, piper at the gates of dawn, who was demonized by the Church, which foolishly projected their Satan, personification of evil, onto him.

Like the Goddess Diana, he unifies opposites as hunter and hunted – reminding us that we too are part of the circle of life and death. Like our ancestors, we may hunt, kill and eat animals but we too are their prey as we are the prey of time. The Horned God binds us to our animal brothers and sisters and reminds us of our dependence on them and also our obligation to them: they sacrifice their lives so we can live. He also reminds us that we too are part animal, a part full of forgotten wisdom without which we can never be fully human or sacred.

As all shamans know, there's divine wisdom, power and magic in the animal parts of ourselves and in the animals who nourish our body and our spirit. They are our guides and teachers – not only in the Other World but also in this one. Cats, dogs, horses and more are our companions in life, and they visit us from the wildness of Nature. If you pay attention, if you ask, they will show you how to trust and follow your instincts, the instantaneous knowledge that can save and change your life.

The Horned God will restore the full measure of joy, power and pleasure of your body and your sexuality. The world is full of magic and divinity, but you need the part of you that is animal to sense it, to fully appreciate and enjoy it. The Horned God will guide you. Call Him and He will come. He will lead you in the dance of your embodied spirit, but be prepared to be challenged and changed.

Practice: Dancing with the Horned God

You may wish to use a set of deer antlers, or a bull's horn, as a symbol of the Horned God. The chant Lord of the Dance *is to the well-known tune* Tis a Gift to be Simple, *which you can listen to online and sing in this rite of communion.*

Let's begin.

1. Late at night, when the Moon is high and the stags move freely, preferably outside, in your place of power, cast your circle.

2. Call the Horned God, saying: *'By hoof and by horn I call you, By hide and by bone I call you, by sinew and by muscle I call you. Come to me, dance with me, bless me with the gift of remembering the holy wisdom of my body.'*

3. Begin by moving slowly. Stomp your feet on the ground, lower your head and raise it; feel your antlers, your horns, sprouting, crowning your head. Feel the power of the stag, the bull, the goat coming to you. Feel the presence and the power of the Horned God, regardless of your gender. Dance and feel his joy. Dance and feel His gentleness, His kindness and generosity. He will give you His life; He will fill you with life.

4. Dance, dance, dance and sing *The Lord of the Dance*: *'Dance, dance, wherever you may be, for I am the Lord of the Dance said He, and I'll lead you all, wherever you may be, I will lead you all in the Dance, said He.'*

5. Sing and dance until you fall upon the ground, breathless, joyful, empowered. Feel His energy coursing through you. When you feel Him withdrawing, bow your head and thank Him.

6. Ground, eat and drink something. Close your circle, go home and get a good night's sleep. Pay attention to your dreams. Write about your experience in your magical journal.

God embodied

God is not an idea. He is not abstract, transcendent or unknowable. To some extent, our humanity limits our ability to fully know the Divine – there will always be Mystery to seek. But there's a God who dwells within. He reminds us that our humanity is the expression of divinity. A living, present God grounds you in the magic of *your* life. You embody Him, just as you embody Her, as you embody divinity beyond gender or polarity. Invite Him into your life and He will come, shining with light, covered in green leaves, bearing wisdom meant just for you and for all the world, playing pipes and dancing in ecstasy.

Chapter 9

The Wheel of the Year

'...all that falls shall rise again!' Without signal and all at once, the laughter, chanting and dancing stopped. Dozens of us gazed up at the rainbow of colored ribbons ecstatically woven around the wooden pole. It touched the Sun above us and reached deep into the Earth beneath us.

Silently, breathlessly, prayerfully we stepped closer in, kneeling, stretching, resting our hands upon the World Tree, the axis mundi, *feeling the energy flowing and the magic that we had made together.*

The eight Wiccan Sabbats

Laughter and poetry, beauty and creativity, rejoicing and reflection are what I experience celebrating the Sabbats, the Wiccan calendar of sacred days. Sabbat rituals attune us to all the ways that Nature nourishes, transforms and renews Spirit, and *our* spirits.

Approximately every six weeks, the Wheel of the Year turns to reveal another aspect of Nature's embodied divinity and spiritual wisdom. There are layers of meaning, metaphor and myth within the Sabbats, but at the center of the spinning Wheel is an unchanging revelation: Nature's process of continuous renewal. The forms change but the Spirit that creates is constant.

The Wheel of the Year

The Sabbats honor the Earth's agricultural cycle, and as we celebrate, we attune ourselves and our lives to that profound rhythm. We learn to create, cultivate, reap and release to make room in our lives for the next stage of soul flourishing. Working in harmony with Nature, we come into harmony with Divine energies, unlocking the wisdom and power, fulfillment and peace that come from living in accord with the circle of Life.

Wiccans generally refer to the Sabbats by their Celtic names, but similar sacred calendars were found throughout Europe and the Fertile Crescent of the Middle East and are often adapted in contemporary Sabbat celebrations. And because these are rites honoring the rhythms of Earth and Sun, they have elements in common with Indigenous cultures across the globe, especially those with similar climates and ecosystems.

Four of the Sabbats celebrate the Earth's agricultural cycle:

❖ **Samhain** (popularized as Halloween or All Hallow's Eve)

❖ **Imbolc** (which survived as St. Brigid's Day and Groundhog Day)

❖ **Beltaine**, or May Day (still widely celebrated in Scandinavia)

❖ **Lughnasadh**, or Lammas (still celebrated in Ireland)

The other Sabbats celebrate the four great solar events:

❖ **Yule**, or Winter Solstice

* **Oestara**, or Spring Equinox (named for the Germanic Goddess of Spring, the root of Easter)

* **Litha**, or Summer Solstice

* **Mabon**, or Autumn Equinox

The spiritual wisdom of the seasonal cycle was so deeply rooted in the human experience that parallels can be found in the Abrahamic calendar and were integrated into the Christian holidays.

The dance of love

Goddess and God, Lover and Beloved, the non-gendered terms my tradition often uses, personify a divine partnership. Wiccan Sabbats celebrate this love story, embodied by Earth and Sun. Together, their energy and love spin the Wheel of Creation, an eternal dance revealed and participated in throughout the year, year after year.

The Witches' Sabbats have been grotesquely distorted by Christianity: the sexually repressed and misogynistic projections of the Church imagined wild orgies under the lustful gaze of Satan. These were *not* the reality of the sacred rites of *wicce* and *wicca* and our other Indigenous ancestors.

The Greeks called this divine union the *hieros gamos*, the sacred marriage, a term used by Jungians to refer to the inner union of feminine and masculine aspects of the self. Each Sabbat explores a stage of their relationship as Goddess and God enter the realm of form, are born, live, age, die and are reborn by the eternal power of love. It is the dance of life choreographed through the cycle of the seasons.

Within their love story is another – the 'hero's journey' described by the American mythologist Joseph Campbell – that is at the heart of all the world's faiths. It's a universal tale of enlightenment by descent and death, challenge and transformation, return and rebirth undertaken by, among others, Inanna, Persephone, Isis, Tammuz, Adonis, Dionysus and Osiris, described in the Egyptian Sirius cycle, the Greek Eleusinian Mysteries, the Nordic and Celtic traditions and similar sacred stories of Indigenous peoples across the globe. Even the Abrahamic and Eastern faiths tell the tale of this archetypal journey by Moses, Jesus and Buddha. It's the sacred story of all life on Earth.

It's *your* heroic story too. When you celebrate the Sabbats, you're participating in the great love story of life, death and rebirth that's constantly occurring in the natural world. Sabbat rites that attune you to the Earth and Sun's great cycle of creation, destruction and re-creation, bring your inner and outer world into harmony with the natural world that surrounds and sustains you, the divine context that gives deep meaning and real magic to our lives. Harness those energies and you become your own hero.

Working with the magic of the Wheel

Sabbat rites, revelations and rejoicing bring your body, mind and spirit into rhythm with the sacred world in which we all live. Celebrating awakens you to the magic of the natural world around you and within you.

The Wheel of the Year (*see page 162*) is an annual journey of self-discovery, and once again, Nature is your spiritual guide. The Sabbats offer a cosmic template for a deep harmony and peacefulness in the midst of the successes and losses of life. You learn to harness skillfully the great ebb and flow of seasonal energies and wisely direct your own energies to achieve more easily the life you long for.

Rather than working against the natural flow of the seasons, you participate in and work *with* them. Sabbat rites harness the magic of Creation to nourish your dreams, turn them into realities and reap the rewards, learn from and release your failures, and move on to manifesting new visions in whatever areas of your life you choose – love, health, work, wisdom and more.

Working with the Wheel of the Year transforms, enlightens and empowers your life.

A simple and joyful way to begin is by setting and working to accomplish a goal in sync with the seasons. You're going to work with the Sabbat cycle to plant the seeds of your dreams, to cultivate them, harvest them, honor, celebrate and share them, reflect, rest and begin again.

Working with the Wheel

You can begin at any point during the year, but Samhain is a natural starting point.

❖ Because all new life begins with a dream, begin at Samhain to rest in the darkness and incubate your dream.

❖ At Yule, state your dream aloud and it will light your way forward.

❖ Celebrate its first stirrings within you at Imbolc, and its first appearance in the world at Oestara (Spring Equinox).

❖ Nurture and celebrate it at Beltaine, rejoice in its creative vitality (and yours) at Litha (Summer Solstice).

❖ Celebrate the first fruits at Lughnasadh.

❖ Harvest your efforts at Mabon (Autumn Equinox) and enjoy the fruits of your labor, offering thanks and letting go of whatever you've outgrown.

❖ And as the Wheel comes round to Samhain again, rest, reflect and when you're ready, seek a new vision.

Be sure to record your rites and insights, challenges and achievements in your magical journal. And remember to attend to the wisdom of where you live on Mother Earth. Your Sabbats should reflect the reality of your natural environment and climate.

The North American and Northern European seasonal rhythm is reversed if you're in the Southern Hemisphere, or may be better replaced by the Greek, Italian, Middle Eastern, Egyptian or Indigenous seasonal wisdom. Wiccans work with the spirits of place but are always respectful and careful to not appropriate Indigenous religious traditions.

The spirits of the land will guide you. I had a fruitful conversation with a Yoruban priest whose African ancestors were slaves forcibly brought to America. His practice was to honor the spirits of where he lived and also to honor his ancestors and their traditions as he was taught – a useful lesson for those of us who no longer reside in our ancestral homeland.

A general-purpose Sabbat incense

Grind together equal parts (one tablespoon) of patchouli, sandalwood, orris, rose, fennel, thyme and vervain and a few drops of benzoin and pennyroyal oils. Adjust to suit your nose.

Celebrating the Sabbats

Sabbat rites follow a similar, basic structure that you're becoming familiar with by casting circle. They're not some formal, cast-in-stone ritual executed by someone whom you passively observe. *You* create them, *you* participate in them and *you* make them powerful and meaningful.

If you're called to explore a Sabbat as part of your personal quest, rather than as part of a love story, that's perfectly appropriate. If you want to honor a specific spirit of place, or a phase of the Sun's progress or the Earth's blessings, that's what you should do.

We're rediscovering and recreating these ancient rites and they must be relevant to us, to the spiritual needs we have now, to the wisdom and needs of the Earth now. The use of Beloved and Lover, rather than just Goddess and God, is an example. Gender is just one way in which we perceive and express the innate and creative polarity of the cosmos, but there are many diverse and variable expressions.

I've used Goddess and God in the Sabbat template below, in part because I believe it's important to honor the Goddess and to heal the unhealthy imbalance created by Her suppression, but feel free to use other titles if you prefer. With regard to which Goddesses and Gods to honor, some Wiccan traditions work with a specific pantheon of divinities, but my own Tradition of Ara encourages you to listen for the call of the patron deity/deities and the spirits of place, who will guide you as you work with them.

Each passing year affords more research about Euro-Indigenous traditions, practices and surviving folk wisdom, rites and celebrations that you may wish to integrate when creating your own celebrations. There are also universal labels like Mother, Father, Mother Earth, Father Sun, Lover and Beloved and others that express the energies of the Sabbat and are wonderful to use.

A Sabbat template

Rather than give you a script to follow, I want to encourage your creativity and confidence, so what follows is a template with the essential guidelines to help you create powerful and personally meaningful Sabbat celebrations.

The seasonal wisdom, Goddess, God and other divine aspects, activities, dances, symbols, colors, offerings, chants and more are provided for each Sabbat. There's also language describing the purpose of each Sabbat that you're welcome to use until you feel ready to write your own.

And remember, there are no mistakes, just opportunities to learn. If you're having fun, you're doing it right. Sabbats are filled with rejoicing, play and creativity. Even the most somber rite of Samhain, where we honor our ancestors and loved ones who have passed over, is filled with gratitude and love. Whenever possible, hold your Sabbat outdoors. Use the Table of Correspondences (*see pages 80–81*) to help create your celebration.

Sabbat rites step by step

1. Determine the appropriate colors for the Sabbat. Gather the appropriate seasonal and sacred symbols and expressions. Prepare a libation and bread or cake.

2. Reflect on the divine attributes, personifications and dynamics of the season.

3. Set up your altar using the appropriate objects, symbols and representations of deity. Wear seasonal colors.

4. Purify yourself and the space. Breathe and ground.

5. Cast your circle.

6. Honor the spirit of the place.

7. Declare the meaning of the Sabbat – include guidance you've received from the spirit of the place.

8. Honor/invoke/invite the seasonal Goddess, God, divinity. A simple, heartfelt, poetic invitation addressing them in their seasonal aspect will work beautifully.

9. Celebrate with seasonally appropriate activity or magic. Use seasonal dances and chants, surviving folk practices and your own creativity; divination; journeying; sharing remembrances; journaling. Celebrate with feasting, storytelling, playing games. Specific suggestions for each Sabbat are given below.

10. Thank the Goddess, God, divinity, ancestors and spirit of the place and close circle. End with the parting words:

> *'Our circle is open, but never broken. Merry meet*
> *and merry part and merry meet again.'*

If you're celebrating with others, hugs and kisses all round. If you're working outdoors, leave an offering and leave the place better than you found it. The liquid in the libation bowl should be poured into a moving body of water, or onto the ground. If that's not possible, give thanks as it goes down the drain.

11. Take time before and after your rites to observe the natural world around you. What's happening with the weather, the land, the plants, animals, birds and insects? What do you see, smell, hear, feel? How are things changing around you? Inside you? In your life? How is your life coming into sync with the energies of the season? What have you learned? Write about your observations in your magical journal. Reflect on the lessons you're learning.

Samhain, or Celtic New Year

Pronounced Sow' en; 31 October Northern Hemisphere, 1 May Southern Hemisphere

Purpose

This is the night when the veil between the worlds is thinnest, when we honor and visit with our ancestors, and when we enter the Dreamtime to seek a dream of new life. We open our hearts and open our circle and welcome those we love and have lost, and our ancestors who have wisdom to share with us.

In this time outside of time, this place between the worlds, call to your ancestors, to those you love who have passed. Ask them to be with you, speak with you, advise you and celebrate the love and Spirit that survives even as the forms of life change.

Colors

Black, purple, gold, orange.

Altar

Photographs of people or pets you love or honor who have passed, and objects belonging to them; a pomegranate, the symbol of Persephone; offerings of food and drink for the spirits and a divination tool to speak with them; a drum.

Presiding deities

Any of the 'dark' Goddesses or Gods of death and rebirth. Though Greek, Hecate, the Crone Goddess of Magic and Transformation, guides all those who pass through the Underworld, and Persephone, Maiden and Queen of the Underworld and Hades as Master of Time and the shamanic Underworld (the realm of Spirit, not the Christian hell) are often invoked at Samhain.

Celebrate

After you've cast circle, declared the purpose of the Sabbat and invoked divinity, stand in the West and create an opening – simply move your hand in a counterclockwise circle. Sit and use one of the consciousness-altering techniques you've mastered to deepen your awareness, like breathing, grounding, chanting and drumming in the tempo of a heartbeat.

Feel the veil parting and your loved ones coming to be with you. Welcome them. Use a method of divination, which you'll learn about in Chapter 12, and ask for a message, or simply write in your magical journal as you feel your ancestors communicating with you.

Ask for advice, express your love and gratitude, share whatever you wished to say but didn't when they were alive. Listen carefully for their answers. You will feel them withdraw when the time has come to depart. Thank them. Close the portal in the West. Feast, share remembrances and stories if you're with others, toast your ancestors and give thanks for your life and any guidance you've received. Cut open the pomegranate and eat some of the seeds.

Samhain is also a good Sabbat to seek a vision of a past life or a vision for your future. Use your divination tools (*see Chapter 12*) to see the past and to receive a dream for you new life. Write what you learn in your magical journal.

Chant

'We all come from the Goddess, and to Her we shall return, like a seed of life, dreaming deep within the Earth.'

When you're done, honor and thank your ancestors. Thank the Goddesses and Gods who have guided you and close circle. Keep a dream journal between Samhain and Yule (Winter Solstice).

Yule, or Winter Solstice

20 or 21 December Northern Hemisphere, 20 or 21 June Southern Hemisphere

Purpose

The longest night, when the Goddess – the womb of the cosmos – gives birth to the light. The Sun is reborn, the light grows stronger from this day forward until Summer Solstice. Rejoice that the light returns, honor the Great Mother as the infinite womb nurturing all potentiality into being, including our dreams. Name and honor the dream of new life that you have found since Samhain.

Colors

White, red, green and gold.

Altar

Devote your altar to the Great Mother and the Returning Light. Decorate it with pine boughs, holly, mistletoe. Place a large yellow candle as a symbol of the God, the returning Sun, within a cauldron or large bowl as a symbol of the Goddess, Mother and Womb of Creation.

Presiding deities

The Great Mother, the reborn Sun/Son, the Wise Crone as midwife of new life, the Holly King whose power peaks at this Sabbat, and the Oak King who is reborn.

Celebrate

Inscribe a candle in the color of your goal/dream with your name and your goal. Place it on the altar. Light the yellow Sun candle in the Goddess's cauldron/bowl and recognize your own powers to bring your dreams into being. Feel the love and nourishment of the Mother surrounding you. Feel the light of a new project shining within you. Sing/chant and dance about the altar, holding your candle and charging it with your powers of joy, love and rebirth.

Chant as you dance (see below). When you feel the energies peak, light your candle and hold it aloft, speaking your wish/dream/goal for the new year. Place the candle in a holder and when you're ready to close circle, blow it out and make your wish. Continue with the template steps above, rejoice, give thanks, close. Keep your candle on your altar or somewhere safe to use at Imbolc.

Chant

> *'Bless the Mother who gives birth, Bless our lives upon this Earth, Above us see the Sun returning, feel within the fires burning.'*

Imbolc, or In the belly

Pronounced Im' olk; 2 February Northern Hemisphere, 2 August Southern Hemisphere

Purpose

The holy day of the Goddess Brigid, Imbolc means 'in the belly' in Gaelic and refers to the quickening – the first sign of life stirring within the pregnant sheep. This Sabbat celebrates the life that is now beginning to stir and take shape – within ourselves and within the Earth.

On Imbolc the community came together to lift everyone's spirits with poetry and music, remembering that we're strongest in community – supplies are low at this time of year, but when we gather together, there's enough for everyone. Many small candles create one great light. If you're alone, honor your creative gifts.

Colors

Orange, yellow, red.

Altar

Devote this to the Great Mother and the Growing Light. Use lots of candles, including a yellow Sun candle placed in the Goddess cauldron/bow, your offering, something related to your goal and the blessings of Brigid.

Presiding deities

The Celtic Goddess Brigid, muse to poets and artists, Goddess of fire, sacred wells, healing and smithcraft (creation of civilization), and the God who grows within Her; Taliesin, the mythical Irish poet.

Celebrate

Cast circle, state purpose and invoke Brigid/divinity. Place eight candles evenly spaced around the perimeter of your circle. Starting in the East, light them. Take your candle from Yule and light it from the Sun candle in the cauldron.

Hold it as you chant (see below). When you feel the energy peak, declare you goal and say: *'I offer my light to the world!'* Place the candle on the altar. Create or make your offering if it's already done: write a poem or a short piece honoring your dream, your fire and the nourishment of the Goddess who keeps the flame alive. Read it aloud. Place it on your altar.

Encourage yourself, and those in circle with you, to make your dreams come true. Celebrate with music, laughter, storytelling or journaling if you're alone. When you've closed circle, take your candle and carry it around the circle saying: *'Fire seal the circle round let it fade beneath the ground, let all things be as they were since the beginning of time.'* Blow out all the candles as you walk. Leave your candle burning on the altar – *safely* – until it's gone.

Chant

'I am light, in a circle of light. I am fire burning, burning bright.'

Oestara, or Spring Equinox

Pronounced Ohstar' ah; 20, 21 or 22 March Northern Hemisphere, 20, 21 or 22 September Southern Hemisphere

Purpose

Life returns! Celebrate the magic of life re-emerging from Mother Earth after a winter of frozen sleep. Honor the perfect balance between day and night, light and dark, as the Wheel turns toward light, life and growth. Hope is rewarded as Goddess and God return to life/emerge and our dreams begin to appear in the world. Feel the energy of the Earth moving through you and into the world.

Colors

Green, yellow, purple, pink.

Altar

Symbols of Spring: eggs, images of rabbits, Spring flowers; images of youthful deity; basket of seeds; pots filled with soil if you're indoors, or a hand spade if outside.

Presiding deities

Oestara, Ostara or Eostra (the Anglo-Saxon Goddess of dawn and Spring); Dionysus; the Green Man; Maiden Goddess and Young God; deities as children.

Celebrate

Clear the way with Spring-cleaning – give away outgrown clothes, objects from the past that you're ready to release, habits you're ready to break. Celebrate outdoors if you can. Pay attention to all the signs of life returning, of plants emerging, birds singing, the warmth of the Sun, the softening of the Earth.

Fill the Goddess's cup or cauldron with seeds. When you're ready, cast circle and rejoice in the energies of new life returning and the new life you're creating for yourself. Dance. If you're with others, do the traditional Equinox dance, the Grand Allemande: two interweaving circles, half going clockwise, the other half counterclockwise, taking right hands, then left, then right, etc., as you pass one another.

Chant as you dance. Charge the seeds with your joy and energy. When you feel the energy peak, direct it into the seeds. Plant them and continue chanting. When the second wave of chanting energy peaks, water the seeds. Rejoice, reflect and be sure to leave an offering. Nourish your seed, within and in the Earth.

Chant

'One thing becomes another, in the Mother, in the Mother.'

Beltaine, or May Day

Pronounced Bell' tane; 1 May Northern Hemisphere,
31 October Southern Hemisphere

Purpose

Goddess and God, Lover and Beloved join in love and the Earth blossoms in ecstasy. Celebrate their union, embodied by life and by us. The Sun is warm, the Earth blossoms in beauty. The dance of desire weaves destinies together.

Colors

All the colors, and select one in particular that represents your goal.

Altar

Flowers and early spring fruits and vegetables, ribbons. Make a garland or circlet of flowers, which can decorate the altar, or which you can wear. Images of deities. Or you can simply use the Maypole without an altar.

Presiding deities

Maturing Maiden and Youth; Lady of the Flowers and Lord of the Dance.

Celebrate

Celebrate outdoors and with others if you can. Traditionally, people dance the Maypole. If you're alone, you can weave ribbons together, chanting as you do, and then wrap them around your wand, staff or a large branch. Or if you have a group of friends who might not be ready for a Maypole, ask them to help you in planting a small tree.

You'll need a minimum of a dozen folks for the traditional Maypole; have everyone bring a ribbon that's 20ft (6m) long and at least 1in (2.5cm) wide in the color of the magic they are working on, which you'll tie to the top of the Maypole (which is 8–20ft/5–6m high). Dig a small hole into which the pole is placed and held by at least two people.

Everyone holds their ribbon as they dance the Grand Allemande: people stand back to back in couples, evenly placed at the perimeter of the circle. At the signal to begin, those facing clockwise lift their ribbons as they move forward (*deosil*). Those facing/moving counterclockwise (*widdershins*) duck beneath the ribbons as they move forward. The *widdershins* circle then lifts their ribbons and the *deosil* group ducks under.

Everyone continues dancing, lifting then lowering, raising their own then ducking beneath the oncoming ribbons, weaving over and under until the Maypole is wrapped. Expect a good amount of confusion and laughter, especially as you get closer and closer around the pole. As you dance, chant. Let the power and joy build and grow. When the ribbons are too short for even one more step, tie them off and everyone places their hands on the pole, feeling the energy running between Earth and Sky.

Look at the beauty that surrounds you. Send energy to Mother Earth and thank Her for Her blessings. Feel the incredible power, *your* power, giving shape and form to your goal. Feel your joy and love coursing through you and into the world. Spend the rest of the day with someone you love, or if you're alone, love yourself. The Maypole can be kept as a power object and rewoven next year.

Chant

> *'Corn and grain, corn and grain. All that falls shall rise again. Hoof and horn, hoof and horn, all that dies shall be reborn.'*

You can interweave this chant with a counterpoint Goddess chant:

> *'Isis, Astarte, Diana, Hecate, Demeter, Kali, Inanna' and God chant: 'Pan, Woden, Baphomet, Cernunnos, Osiris.'*

Litha, or Summer Solstice

*Pronounced Li' tha; 20, 21 or 22 June Northern
Hemisphere, 20, 21 or 22 December Southern Hemisphere*

Purpose

This is the longest day, when the Sun is strongest and life on Earth grows abundantly, but from this day forward the light diminishes. The Sun and Earth express the loving union of God and Goddess, Lover and Beloved, entwined at the height of their life-generating powers.

Celebrate and give thanks for the blessings of your life, experience the power of the creative energies manifesting in the world around you and within you. Honor your capacities, your talents and your determination to create the life you want. As the Earth transforms the Sun's energies into life, so we transform the light and divinity within ourselves into goals that will also come to life. Give thanks to Mother Earth for the abundance She gives with complete generosity and thanks for all the blessings in your life.

Colors

Green and yellow, brown and red.

Altar

Fill it to overflowing with seasonal, local fruits, vegetables and flowers, especially roses – the flower represents the Earth's beauty and the thorns the pain of the Sun's departure. An object that symbolizes the goal you're nourishing.

Presiding deities

Mother Goddess of the Fertile Earth, Mature God of the Shining Sun and Oak King at their zeniths of power; you may also wish to use specific Goddesses such as Sovereignty, Ceres and Demeter and Sun Gods such as Lugh, Helios and Sol.

Celebrate

Celebrate outdoors! Lie on the Earth and absorb the life-generating energies of Sun and Earth. Feel the movement of energy into matter, dreams into form. Journey to the point where the shape-shifting occurs, or visit with the spirit of the land at this moment of vitality and growth.

Dance a spiral dance to honor the Sun's descent and the Earth's increasing fertility. Take hands and lead the group, or if you're alone, dance, spiraling *deosil* in toward the altar. Chant the names of Sun Gods and Earth Goddesses. When you reach the altar, turn and begin moving outward in the opposite direction, *widdershins*, passing those who are still moving inward. When you reach the perimeter of the circle, turn and move *deosil* back inward until everyone is circled together around the altar.

Send your energies together into the symbols of your goals for a fruitful manifestation. Litha is a powerful

Sabbat for prosperity, so you can ask the Sun to carry obstacles and poverty away with him and ask Mother Earth to reward your hard work with abundance.

There's a traditional consecration for the wine, symbolizing the divine marriage or union of Goddess and God, Lover and Beloved, said while plunging the athame into the cup: *'Spear to cauldron, lance to Grail, spirit to flesh, flesh to spirit, Lover to Beloved, God to Goddess, Sun to Earth. We give thanks for all the blessings this union brings.'*

Lughnasadh, or Lammas

Pronounced Loo' nesa or Loo' na sod; Lammas is pronounced Lah' mahs; 1 August, or halfway between Summer Solstice and Autumn Equinox, Northern Hemisphere; February 1, 2, or halfway between Winter Solstice and Spring Equinox, Southern Hemisphere

Purpose

The celebration of the beginning of the harvest, honoring the God Lugh with the offering of 'first fruits,' games, dancing and rejoicing, this Gaelic tradition is both a funeral and a celebration of life that continues today throughout Ireland.

The rites marked the cutting of the first grain with offerings of thanks to the land, the spirits and deities for the first fruits, and offerings for the protection of the crops that were still ripening. There are games and competitions, dances and horse races, trips to sacred wells, bonfires and the baking and consuming of bread.

Colors

Green, brown, yellow.

Altar

Lammas means Feast of Bread so this should be the main feature, in addition to seasonal, local fruits, grains, corn, vegetables and flowers. Also, the symbol of your goal, your harvest.

Presiding deities

Mother Earth; Goddess Tailtiu and her son Lugh, God of Grain; the Green Man.

Celebrate

Bake bread and place it on your altar. After your rite, take some to a food pantry (food bank) as an offering. Give thanks for the blessings of Mother Earth and for the blessings of the departing Sun.

Cut a piece of corn from its sheath, wheat from its stalk, or a chunk of bread from the loaf and say: *'We give thanks for the gift of the Mother, the Green God who sacrifices himself so that we may live, and that He may live again. We honor the balance and know that for all that is given, something must be returned. We give thanks for the nourishment, patience and strength for the harvest ahead.'*

Eat and enjoy and leave some as an offering. Pour your libations directly onto the Earth with thanks to the Mother. This is also a great Sabbat for dancing and games.

Chant

See Litha chant.

Mabon, or Autumn Equinox

Pronounced Mab' on; 20, 21 or 22 September Northern Hemisphere, 20, 21, or 22 March Southern Hemisphere

Purpose

Celebration of the Great Harvest, giving thanks for the Earth's generosity, abundance and blessings; recognition of the perfect balance of day and night, light and dark that now inclines toward the dark Winter ahead. We're reminded to share with others so that we may all be sustained through difficult times. Celebrate outside!

Colors

Green, orange, yellow, red.

Altar

Pile high with the autumnal local harvest of flowers, fruits and vegetables – if possible, an ear of corn still on its stalk – and a sickle, symbolizing the harvest and the Crone. Also, images of Goddess as Crone and God as Wise Elder.

Presiding deities

Mother Earth; Crone Goddess Hecate; Lugh as Grain/ Corn God; Wise Old God as Holly King, eternally green.

Celebrate

Make an offering to give thanks for your harvest and all the blessings you've received during the year. Reflect on the aspects of your life that no longer serve your growth and happiness. Write them on a piece of paper.

You can raise energy with the Equinox dance if you're with others, the Grand Allemande (see Spring Equinox), or spiraling yourself while chanting (see Litha). When the energy peaks, take a candle and light your paper with what you're releasing and toss it into the cauldron as an offering to the fires of transformation.

In my tradition, the oldest woman, representing the Crone Goddess, enters the circle, holds the corn stalk in one hand and the sickle in the other and says: *'We are blessed by the fruits of Sun and Earth. Here is the Mystery revealed: Though the form changes, the energy of life is eternal. The Sun has gone into the seed!'*

As she finishes, she cuts the corn from the stalk and holds it aloft, which usually provokes cheers. You can do and say this yourself if you're celebrating alone. Tear up or burn the paper with what you are releasing. Eat the corn as your libation and leave some as an offering for the animals.

Chant

See Litha. Chant with a counterpoint of Z. Budapest's:

'We all come from the Goddess, and to Her we shall return, like a drop of rain flowing to the ocean.'

The turning Wheel

As the Wheel of the Year completes a cycle, take out your magical journal and read about your journey of change and fulfillment. Reflect on how much you've accomplished, what you've outgrown and relinquished and what you've learned about yourself, the natural world and Spirit during this great cycle of transformation. And ask yourself, what comes next?

Renewal

Celebrating the Sabbats unites you with the natural world in which you live, with your ancestors and your community which is growing beyond the human family. As the Wheel turns and you rejoice with Nature, you'll discover the deep spiritual rhythm and love story of your own life. Joining the eternal dance of the Earth and Sun, you'll discover that, in the face of the greatest challenges, you possess the power of renewal, the power to create and to re-enchant your life and the world.

Chapter 10

Spellcasting

'Star light, star bright... I wish I may, I wish I might, have this wish I wish tonight.'

I was five years old, holding my mother's hand as I searched the evening sky for the first star to appear. I remember the happiness I felt when I spotted it. I remember repeating the nursery rhyme. I remember the excitement as I sent my wish to a universe that I knew was alive. And I remember that my wish came true.

I had found the place inside myself where anything was possible.

Remember the power of your childhood wishes made on a star, blowing out the candles on your birthday cake, or sending a letter to Santa? Remember the fairy tales and story books, TV shows, movies and online games featuring Witches and wizards, fairy godmothers and magicians, and even little girls and boys fighting demons, riding dragons and wearing ruby red slippers? You learned that the power had been inside of you all along.

We're adults now, but we still long for that feeling and that power. We long for an affirmation to repeat, a wand to wave, a spell to chant that will make our dreams come true. But by now you know what it takes for *real*, *divine* magic to manifest. And it's a lot easier, and simpler, than most people think.

People usually think a spell is a set of secret words that will, with special timing and ingredients, make magic for them. And the words usually rhyme. The last part is true – a spell is an incantation, an enchantment: words that originally meant singing a charm.

In almost every religious tradition, letters and language, images and symbols have sacred and magical power and Wicca is no different. And it turns out that what our spellcasting ancestors knew is being proven by modern science – rhyming has a powerful and positive effect on the listener's mind, emotions and inclinations. In other words, spells alter your consciousness. And as you've already experienced, when you alter your consciousness, magic begins to manifest.

Spellcasting takes us to the place inside where anything is possible. In that sacred place within, magic awakens and we're able to make things happen in our lives and in the world. But as we explored in the chapter on magic, it doesn't work the way most people, including a lot of Wiccans and Witches, think it does...

Spellcasting step by step

I was taught the basic approach to spellcasting that most people continue to practice today:

1. Cast circle as a container for your energy.

2. Visualize and create a 'thought form' of your desired outcome in precise detail, also called 'setting your intention' (on the 'Akashic plain,' an energy plain or field of pure potential).

3. Invoke/ask the relevant deity or elemental spirit to aid you.

4. Raise energy by chanting the spell, dancing or other ecstatic practices.

5. Use your willpower to direct the energy into a cone of power (the point where energy 'peaks' above the altar) and from there into your thought form.

6. Visualize your goal manifesting.

7. Believe it will happen and act in accord by taking necessary actions in daily life to make your intention a reality.

8. Don't talk about the spell for at least 24 hours, to prevent doubt or tinkering from interfering with the spell you've set in motion.

Sometimes this approach works. But often it doesn't, leaving people wondering why not. Just as when the

Law of Attraction doesn't work, they wonder if they didn't believe deeply enough. Did they let doubt creep in and spoil the spell? Maybe they didn't use the right ingredients or do it at the right time of the month; or perhaps they need another spell, a new script, a different rhyme? Are there secrets they didn't know?

There are, and if you've skipped ahead to this chapter, hoping to find the simple and easy secrets of successful spellcasting, I'll share them with you now, but you'll have to go back to Chapter 1 to unlock the real power. Here's why:

Mechanical magic

There's a fundamental, even fatal, flaw in the traditional approach to spellcasting. Fix it and you're on your way to a magical life. The old model of magic treats the universe as if it's inanimate matter that we can will into whatever form or manifestation we want. Spells are formulas and the universe a machine – just use the right words, ingredients and gestures, push the button and the cosmic vending machine delivers your goodies. Or, in the really old model, the universe bends to your will and does your bidding.

You cannot make real magic by imposing your will on Creation. That attitude is contrary to the heart and soul of Wicca.

Quantum magic

Isaac Newton's physics explain only part of how the universe works: the part that has created modern wealth *and* destruction. But in the last 100 years, quantum physics has created a paradigm shift in our understanding of reality. We now know that there are more than three dimensions and very different laws of physics operating in those dimensions, perhaps even realms of Spirit.

In quantum reality, everything is interconnected energy that our consciousness and expectations seem to be able to affect. Think it, especially in the altered states of consciousness we've been exploring, and your intention can often manifest.

This is the underlying purpose of meditation with a focus or mantra, and of visualizing, imagining and setting your intention, which are essentials of magic and spells (along with affirmations and the Law of Attraction). Raising energy and other ecstatic practices also alter your consciousness, your emotions and your physical energies, all of which are required for successful spellcasting.

Wicca and traditional cultures that practice shamanism cultivate spiritual technologies that work with this understanding of altered consciousness and an energetically interconnected reality. When you master practices laid out in *Wicca Made Easy* that generate heightened states of awareness and sensitivity achieved by *wicce*, shamans, yogis, healers and others, you too can have a remarkable, transformative and healing impact on the outcome of events. In a very real sense, spellcasting is quantum magic.

But as you expand your awareness and open your heart, you'll discover that you are not living within a merely quantum mechanical universe. And we're not the masters of quantum Creation, entitled to impose our altered consciousness and will upon it for our own ends. You require something even more profound than quantum consciousness for real magic and spells to work.

The secret of successful spellcasting

Magic happens when your mind clears, your heart opens and you recognize that Creation is alive and sacred. The energy you work with when you cast a spell is sacred, and so are you. Your thoughts, willpower, feelings and physical exertions are all expressions of divine energy – just as Air, Fire, Water and Earth, *all* of Nature, are expressions of divine energy. When you awaken to, experience and honor the divine energy of life, you'll make real magic and cast spells that work.

**The real secret of successful spellcasting
is your connection to divinity.**

Divine magic and sacred spells

When you cast a spell, you're working in partnership with the *vital, Sacred Source of Creation*. You're also going to the holy well of your own inner divinity, drawing up that energy and giving it shape and form in a sacred world.

A spell is an expression of your own empowerment, rather than the helplessness that often spurs people to pray for the intervention of God. When you cast a spell for love or money, health or inspiration, peace or empowerment, you're expressing your faith in yourself, and in Creation, to create the life you deserve – a life in which you're able to fulfill your potential, your passions, your purpose. A spell is an expression of your own sacred power to make that life, in harmony and partnership with the divinity of the world of which you're an integral part.

Casting spells is just one way of making magic, one way of experiencing the magic of Creation, but it's one of the most creative, joyful and artistic. When you cast spells, you become an artist working with the palette of the seen and unseen, of Spirit and Nature, energy and life. Casting spells, you co-create with the Divine, giving shape, beauty and life to its infinite potential.

Spellcasting step by step

So, let's cast a spell.

1. Set your intention

Why are you going to cast your spell? What is your goal? What extra bit of help, healing, strength or creative energy do you need? Is it prosperity, a new job, a new home, a new love? Do you want to get rid of old habits, problems, patterns? What is your vision for your future? What would change if you could manifest magic in your life?

Shamanic practices have always been used for practical, real-world needs – where should someone live or look for love; what was the illness afflicting someone and what would cure it; what was the purpose of someone's life and how should they fulfill it; who were the guardians and guides willing to help someone? They are all appropriate reasons to cast a spell.

2. Sympathetic magic

I love the term. It evokes kinship, a harmony of feeling and natural agreement. Sympathetic magic is the casting of spells using symbols, words and objects that connect your soul to the Divine, and using symbolic actions to manifest your goal. The Green Man magic (Planting seeds of change practice in Chapter 8) was an example: you planted a seed in a pot of soil, took care of it every day and as the seed grew, so did the manifestation of your goal symbolized by the seed and nurtured by your daily meditations, incantations and actions.

Your spell is an artistic, symbolic enactment of your goal using objects and activities that represent or are associated with that goal. This is where the use of power objects, potions, incense, candles, all the props and visuals, come into play (you'll learn about these in Chapter 11).

The Table of Correspondences (*see pages 80–81*) and Chapter 11 provide guidance in choosing your creative palette. Make your list and gather what you'll need to cast your spell – herbs and oils for incenses or potions; candles to carve; a square of fabric; a piece of yarn or ribbons of the appropriate colors; parchment paper and a pen for a talisman, sigil or other writing; ripe fruit and dark chocolate; a loaf of black bread and a thimble of honey; three white feathers found at the beach; the rose quartz necklace your mother wore or a nautilus shell in which you can hear the ocean singing; a silver cup and a black-handled knife; a wand of willow and a copper pentacle. The possibilities are as infinite as your creativity.

You can make magic with anything that captures and expresses your imagination and your growing understanding of Creation's web of connection. And you can cast a spell without anything at all except your mind, courage and heart, your energy and your connection to the Divine.

Spellcasting is both craft and art, and once you've developed your skills and confidence, your knowledge of your palette and yourself, it's a gorgeously creative process. For a spell to work, you need to put yourself into it, which is why as soon as you're ready, you'll write your own script rather than relying on someone else's.

3. Prepare an offering

Reciprocity is a wise law of Nature and therefore magic: give something when you're asking to receive something.

Making an offering reminds you that spellcasting, even when it's about self-care, is never selfish. Your offering should be freely and sincerely made with genuine gratitude and generosity. And an offering related to your spell creates balance and harmony – like making a donation of clothes that no longer fit you to Dress for Success if you're doing magic for a new job or business success.

4. Time your spellcasting

Magic and spellcasting work with Nature's energies and rhythms. You're going to time your spells just the way farmers time their work. They know the cycles of the seasons and the powers of the Moon's phases – they don't plant a seed when they should be harvesting or water when they should weed.

Banishing during a full Moon is like trying to swim against the tide: the energies literally push you, or your goal, in the opposite direction. As you've learned from your Sabbat and lunar rites, working *with* the cycles of the Moon, Earth, Sun and cosmos is like riding a great wave – you'll go further, faster and more easily. With practice, it will become second nature to determine the best time of day, week, season and/or lunar phase to cast your spell or create a ritual:

❖ Waning Moon, and waning solar time of year, are best for banishing, releasing, letting go, changing bad habits, getting rid of unwanted problems, ending bad relationships.

❖ Waxing or full Moon, waxing solar time of year, the middle of the day, when the Sun is high and strong, are best for manifesting, creating, building, growing, setting intentions and acting on them.

❖ Dark Moon, Samhain, the period between Samhain and Yule (Winter Solstice) are particularly good for divination, dreamwork, visiting ancestors, past-life recall, resting and working with the unconscious.

5. Purify

Yourself, your space, your tools and your intention.

6. Cast your circle

See Chapter 6.

7. Honor/invoke divinity

The next step is to acknowledge and feel your connection with divinity. The old phrase is to invoke Goddess or God. It's an invitation for the Sacred to join you in your magical circle and aid you in the spell you're shaping. You draw the Goddess or God, or non-gendered divinity, up from within yourself and invite Her/Him/Them/It to join you from the Other World and from the natural world that surrounds and sustains you.

While traditionally we've related to deity in mostly human terms, Wicca also honors the innate divinity of all of Creation beyond human metaphor and gender. The Table of Correspondences (*see pages 80–81*) and the chapters on Nature, Goddess and God are good starting places for determining which deity or aspect of divinity is most appropriate for the goal of your spell. Communion with divinity, gratitude, respect and reverence are the posture from which to invite the aid of divinity as you cast your spell.

8. Raise energy/receive energy

Spells need energy to work – divine energy from within and without. You need the energies of your own spirit, mind, heart and body. All of the steps thus far open you to receive these energies and help you to raise or generate them.

In addition to those steps, the breathing practices you've mastered connect you to the Air, to the green plants and the divine web of life; grounding connects you to the energy of the Earth; casting circle opens your heart and connects you to the Divine and to others in the circle.

Ecstatic practices like chanting, dancing, running and drumming all alter consciousness, body and soul create a channel to and for natural energies *and* 'raise' physical energy for you to draw upon as you cast your spell. And above all, you need the *right* energy: the energy of divine love.

9. Cone of power/Be the Grail

Direct energies into the cone of power

You'll feel the moment when the energies peak. Traditionally, it's directed through your hands into a visualized 'cone of power' rising over the altar in the circle's center. The energies move into your thought form, the visualization of your spell's goal, on the Akashic or energy plain.

It's like sending a current of energy into the field of infinite potential, or planting a seed in the womb of Creation, and since that field and womb are part of a living sacred Oneness, gratitude, respect, reverence and love are the precondition for sending energy. And I always send some of that energy as an offering, reciprocating for what I'm asking to receive/create.

Holding energies within the Grail

Some of the most important magic and spellcasting you'll ever do is what I call Grail Magic. You're already doing it with meditation, breathing and grounding as you open yourself – body, mind and spirit – to the blessing powers of the Divine.

The energies remain within the circle and within you. You can also direct them to whatever your goal may be: healing, enlightenment, energizing or simply communion. When you're done, when you're rested, recharged and inspired, return the remaining energies to their source, with gratitude. Just as the circle is a cauldron in which you're transformed, you are a Grail in which the Divine makes *its* magic.

10. Set your spell, give thanks, close circle, act in accord

Set your spell

Setting and releasing your spell is like tying the knot at the end of a thread when you're done sewing. It locks your energy and intention into place and releases or sends it off to take form. Another way to set your spell – as long as you approach spellcasting with reverence for the divine energy you're working with – is to use the old phrase *'As I do will, so mote it be.'*

Give thanks

Gratitude is another secret to successful spellcasting. Make your offering before you close circle, and follow through afterward if it involves actions in daily life.

Close circle
See Chapter 6.

Any physical expression of your spell, like a talisman, candle or other expression, should be kept in a place of respect, such as your altar or other safe spot, until the spell is fulfilled, and then it may be returned to the essential elements from which it was originally made, again with thanks.

Act in accord

This is the final step, which most people simply refer to as *Believing*. But it's not enough to believe – spells don't work if you don't work with them. You must take the necessary actions in the world for your spell to manifest. Go back to school and get your degree, start that online business, go see a therapist or file for divorce. You can't expect magic, or a spell, to do for you what you're not prepared to do for yourself. *Your life is your magic.* Act in accord.

Practice: Cast a simple spell for protection

Visualize a sphere of light in the center of your stomach. Feel its energy, heat, power.

Clap and send the sphere out and all around you, covering you from head to toe, shoulder to shoulder and a few inches beyond. Feel the energy, heat, power surrounding you. Nothing can get through it except air and information.

When you no longer need the sphere of protection, reach your arms out, grasp the sphere with both hands and pull it back in to your stomach.

Ethics, magic and spells

Would you pray for something bad to happen to someone? Of course not. And for the same reasons –

you're invoking the Divine – you'd never cast a spell to harm someone. The only difference between prayer and a spell is that, when you cast a spell, you go to the well of your own inner divinity in addition to seeking the aid of a divine power greater than yourself.

Some Wiccans say that the reason not to cast spells to harm others (baneful magic) or to hex someone (a misuse of the word hex as harmful magic) is because of the 'Threefold Law' – what you send out returns to you three times over. I've been challenging this notion for many years. The Threefold Law is *not* a proper basis for Wiccan ethics. Why not? Because it's a rule enforced by punishment – I won't do harm because if I do, I'll experience worse harm myself. In other words, I'll be punished.

It's a remnant of patriarchal thinking – when God isn't present in the world, you need rules to determine right from wrong and rules need to be enforced by the threat of punishment. Break the Ten Commandments and you go to Hell. But behavior motivated by punishment isn't ethical: it's just self-interest in avoiding pain. It's the wrong approach for a spirituality that experiences all of Creation as divine.

My Wiccan ethic is simple: *We seek to live in a sacred manner because we live in, and are part of, a sacred world.* It's the right foundation for right action. And it's the real reason behind another ethical precept often cited by Wiccans: *And you harm none, do what you will.* Why should we do no harm? *Because we live in a sacred world.*

Still, it's not enough simply to refrain from doing harm. Living in a sacred world motivates us to *positive* action. It means living with reverence, respect, gratitude and reciprocity toward others and toward Mother Earth. Living in a sacred world means living in harmony and balance; it means learning to live, as all living things do, in ways that make the world more conducive to life. Living in a sacred world means paying careful attention to and being guided by the wisdom and ways of Nature as it embodies divinity.

We still have a lot to figure out about what it means to live in a sacred manner. For example, seeking justice rather than revenge or deciding whether to eat animals, when and if to go to war or break the law in civil disobedience. These are now conversations we can have from the right premise as we rediscover how to live in a sacred and right relationship with Mother Earth and with each other.

Practice: Cast a simple spell for healing

Cast circle. Sit in the center.

Ground and raise energy from Mother Earth. Direct Her energy to the part of your body, mind, heart, soul that needs healing. Send some of that healing back to Mother Earth, with gratitude. Take consistent action to heal a wound we've inflicted on Mother Earth.

What about spells that don't work?

When a spell works, the world feels utterly magical. But what about when a spell doesn't work? Or it works but with results that aren't what you'd expected or hoped for? Anyone who's cast a love spell knows that they can produce very peculiar results – seemingly perfect until they're not.

Wicca is the Craft of the Wise. There's always wisdom to be found in whatever the outcome of your spell. When you discern the lesson, real magic is unleashed. Self-knowledge leads to self-acceptance *and* to change.

No matter what happens on the outside, magic changes you on the inside. You'll begin to discover that 'everything in life is sacred, both the bitter and the sweet.'

Whether your spell produces the goal you were envisioning or not, the real goal at the heart of all spells is to find the Divine within every situation, and within yourself.

When you're able to do that, you'll realize that the most important thing magic changes is *you*.

Practice: Cast a simple spell for courage

Do something you're afraid of. While you do it, yell: '*As I do will, so mote it be.*'

Open-minded spells

You don't always have to visualize your goal to the last detail. In fact, that can be counterproductive. Over years of spellcasting, I've learned to trust the universe, and I urge you to do the same. Craft an open-minded spell that simply asks for what's best for you. Instead of asking for a Ferrari, which you can't afford and can't enjoy because of speed limits, ask for transportation that will be best for you. And be grateful when you get a 10-speed bicycle for your birthday – it is precisely the thing to help you stave off coronary heart disease.

Practice: Cast a simple spell for prosperity

Get a large green candle. On it, carve your name and a large dollar/ pound/currency sign. Set the candle on a plate full of bay leaves. Light the candle and let it burn.

Repeat this prosperity spell until you feel your inner energies shift and the blessings of abundance, prosperity and generosity of Mother Nature flow to you:

> *'Mother from whom all blessings flow*
> *Help me make my prosperity grow*
> *With work that I love for which I'm well paid*
> *Helping all with all that I have made.'*

Make an offering with a donation of time, energy or something useful to someone who has less than you. Act in accord. Make a gratitude list – one day a week, add something to it for which you're grateful.

The last secret

Spells are personal, creative, religious ritual, a rite of communion and co-creation with a divine, living universe, the art of honoring ourselves and the world as sacred. They are drawn from the well of your inner divinity to give shape and form to your life, and they work best when they are divinely inspired and created with the numinous energy that shapes Creation.

Practice: Cast a simple spell for peace

Light a white candle. Ask for stillness and clarity of mind. Breathe. Thank the trees. Thank Mother Earth.

Spells can be richly elaborate and they can be as simple as opening your heart and wishing on the first star you see tonight. The most important secret of all is that all real spells are, in one way or another, love spells.

Practice: Cast a simple spell for love

Fill your bathtub with warm water, rose oil and red rose petals. Get in and soak. Cry if you need to.

Feel the gentle power of the water that surrounds and embraces you. Feel your heart open and fill with love, like a cup that runs over with abundance. Feel how good it feels for your heart to be filled and to offer it to someone worthy of receiving your love. Feel how good it is to receive love. Float in the feelings of love, joy and gratitude. Love yourself.

When you're done, wrap yourself in a warm robe. Take a few drops of the bath water (without soap) and add it to a large pitcher of clean water. Clean the leaves of your plants and water them as you tell them how much you love them. Write a love letter to yourself, or to those who already love you, and keep it in your magical journal.

Chapter 11

The Craft of the Wise

*'...Hermione raised her wand, moved it in
a circle through the air, and a wreath of
Christmas roses blossomed before them...'*
J.K. ROWLING, *HARRY POTTER AND THE DEATHLY HALLOWS*

*Witches are famous for wands and brooms, cats
and cauldrons and the potions and stuff that goes
in them. Behind the stereotypes are truths about
spiritual energy taking shape and form in the
material world in ways that make life truly magical.*

Talismans and tools, potions and power objects

Spells, ceremony, ritual and other sacred practices for
healing, transformation, manifestation and much more
often work with the divine power of natural and human-
made power objects. This is the *Materia Mystica* (mystical
materials in Latin), the sacred arts and crafts of Wicca

and, once you've banished the stereotypes, it has much in common with other shamanic traditions.

Every natural object is a conductor, a channel, a medium of divinity. Nature's creations, and objects made by us like the Wiccan 'tools of art,' are evocative symbols and more – they *embody* divine energy. When we work with natural or power objects in a sacred manner for a sacred purpose, they occupy liminal space where Spirit and matter are interchanged. They are a bridge between worlds through which divine energies flow.

Spirit moves into and acts upon the world in the form of or through the object and the object itself can be a portal into realms of Spirit. A natural or power object can also be a receptacle or home for Spirit. It can be a guide to how Spirit takes shape and lives in the world and an aid for us to live well in the world.

Everything is energy and part of Wiccan wisdom is an understanding of how that energy is embodied in the material world: how to discern the unique and helping qualities of natural and human-made power objects and how to learn from and work with them.

Wiccan ritual, ceremony, spells and practices rely not only on the powers of your mind or will but also on the wisdom of your body, the gifts of your senses and the divine blessings of the natural world. You're learning to practice a sensual, embodied spirituality that honors the innate powers of Nature to open your consciousness, alter your mood, heal and nourish your body, teach you how to live and inspire your spirit. That is what working with Nature, Her creations and our creations, is all about. This is the craft of Witchcraft.

Hidden meanings

Cauldron

An ancient Celtic symbol of the Goddess Cerridwen, the regenerative womb of the Goddess, source of Life, and vessel of magic and transformation; the Holy Grail.

Cat

A *wicce*'s familiar or animal companion and magical assistant. It doesn't have to be a cat: Webster, my familiar, was a Cairn terrier, a wise and holy teacher.

Broom

Wicce were said to fly on brooms, which seems to go back to the Italian tradition of *la vecchia religione*, the Old Religion, and the use of psychotropics to induce an altered state in which the user experienced magical flight between the worlds. Also used for cleaning and purification.

Pointy hat

There are two theories about the hat – one is that it was a symbol of the cone of power raised during magic, the other is that it was part of the negative depiction of *wicce* to make them appear out of fashion, frumpy and un-hip.

Potions

The creation of healing potions was the foundation for much of modern medicine.

Beauty

One of the most discernable blessings of natural objects is their innate beauty. Mother Nature may make some things that appear weird, but look carefully and everything is astonishingly beautiful. The beauty, artistry and craft of Wiccan rites, practices and objects remove your blindfold and awaken you to the beauty of the world around you, to the divine magic within you and embodied by Nature.

The appreciation and creation of beauty is itself a practice of enlightenment and joy. Wiccan circles and ceremonies are similar to the creation of a Buddhist mandala or a Navajo sand painting – the process is the prayer, the offering, the making of transformative beauty in the moment of creation and then it is swept away as the circle is closed, the altar broken down, the form dissolved back into the world. But we who created and participated are forever transformed. And so we transform the world.

Places, like things, hold energy, and I've always been deeply moved to enter any sacred house of worship. But one of the most empowering and transformative aspects of Wicca is that we 'create' the sacred space, the altar, the beauty in which we immerse ourselves and it can be created anywhere. Wicca is profoundly creative, which means *you* are profoundly creative – from the rituals, spells and magic you'll create to all the objects with which you'll work.

Correspondences

Contemporary Wiccans have developed a sophisticated artistry based upon the energies of herbs, oils, stones, crystals, elements, tools and many other items used in magic. This system of energetic relationships and symbolic meanings is the Correspondences, and you've already been working with them in the classic Table of Correspondences.

Wiccans work with this system because it reflects the climate and geographical realities in which we live (although North and South and the timing of the seasons are the opposite south of the Equator).

It may seem daunting at first, with so much to learn and remember – how to set up the altar, which color candle to use, which herbs to mix – but the more you practice, the easier, more creative and yes, more fun, it gets. Use the Table of Correspondences to guide you, along with the lists in this book and elsewhere (there's a wealth of information everywhere these days, just double check the expertise of the source) as you work with the system of meanings and relationships.

Gradually, this useful wisdom structure will become second nature, and along the way you're likely to find a particular passion, skill or gift that will enrich your life and your spirituality.

The powers of natural objects

Natural and human-made power objects serve many helpful purposes, like healing, divination, invocation, containing, shaping and directing energy, and much more. And not surprisingly, many of the healing, therapeutic and even magical qualities ascribed to the natural objects and the system of Correspondences have been verified by scientific studies. Green Witchery, herbal lore and healing are an essential wisdom tradition within Wicca and much of it managed to survive the Witchcraze to provide the foundation of modern medicine.

We'll explore some of the essentials of how and when to work with tools and talismans, potions and power objects, and, I hope, you'll unlock a spiritual creativity that you may not know you have.

Natural objects include crystals, stones and the elements themselves, as well as gifts from the other children of Mother Earth such as plants (often called herbs), the hides, bones, antlers or other parts of animals like feathers, shells and spiderweb silk. Natural objects already embody divine energy and have their own innate qualities, powers and purposes. If approached properly, they have gifts, blessings and wisdom they will share with us. Very often, all you have to do is ask.

Earthly embodiments

When approached with reverence and respect, everything in Nature has something to teach and offer us. Learning to listen and opening yourself to receive Nature's wisdom is the first step of making magic with natural and human-made power objects.

The old belief about magic was that if you could name something, you could control it. And to some extent, like diagnosing a physical illness or psychological issue, naming something does give you power over it. But when we label something, we also distance ourselves from it – we objectify it and so create the illusion of understanding and control. For example, when you call something a tree, you distance yourself in a superior way, essentially saying to yourself and the tree: 'I know what you are, what a tree is.' But do you really?

I've adapted a wonderful practice called Un-Naming, developed by the eco-psychologist Dr. Michael J. Cohen, that will enable you to discover the real identity, wisdom and blessings of whatever you're interacting and working with. We're going to lift the label and see what you discover underneath.

Practice: Un-Naming

You'll need paper and a pen.

❖ Go outside and allow yourself to be attracted to or called by some natural object or Nature being. It could be a tree, a flower, a rock, the ocean, a branch, a feather, a stone, a shell on the beach.

❖ Ask if it would like to work with you. You know that it's agreeable to working with you if you have a feeling happiness, willingness or warmth in response to your question. If it's an object and you get that positive feeling, pick it up. If you can't go outside, look through the natural objects that you've collected and ask which would like to work with you.

❖ Sit down, close your eyes, relax and breathe. Hold the object in both hands then bring it close to your heart. Or sit in view of it.

❖ You are now going to remove its label, e.g. 'tree.' Describe the tree without using the word 'tree' or oak, apple, pine, branch, leaf, root or any other label. The key to this technique is that to describe the tree, you must ask it to show itself to you, to explain itself to you. Your humility and respect will encourage the tree, or other object and its spirit, to work with you.

❖ Observe. Listen. Pay careful attention. Be patient and open. What is it telling you? Write down the things you observe about this unnamed Mystery, such as:

'A home where birds and squirrels live.'

'A living being that creates oxygen and requires carbon dioxide to live.'

'A being that is strong but which bends in storms...'

❖ When you're finished, thank whatever you've worked with for teaching you about itself. Acknowledge it as a teacher, and thank it for the beauty you're being shown, the wisdom, blessings and joy you're being given.

❖ If you've worked with a natural object, ask if it would like to return home as a power object. If it agrees, keep it on your altar or in a place of care and respect for future work together. Do some reading and research to learn more about your natural teacher. Journal about your experience and your research.

This is a wise way of knowing the world. You'll begin to discover the deep and true nature of what you're looking at and interacting with. And most importantly, you'll start to discern relationships between all the parts of Nature. You'll begin to see and to experience the interconnectedness and interdependence of all life.

Let Nature teach you and you'll discover profound lessons about how we should be living – everything in Nature lives together in relationships based on mutual dependence and balance, in ways that enhance the quality of life for all Life. Nature reveals the wise perfection of divine order, and by living in harmony with Nature, you're living in harmony with divinity. You're also living a magical life because you see the world differently – as the body of the Sacred. And, perhaps for the first time, you're seeing the world clearly. Call it harmonious vibration, if you like.

Plants

Plants are living beings with spirits. In shamanic traditions, it's known that they will work with us as teachers, healers and allies. My encounter with the Green Man, the subject of my next memoir, challenged and deepened the foundations and practices of my spirituality, my reverence for Mother Earth and especially for Her plant children.

There's an entire branch of ancient plant wisdom, called Green Magic, Green Witchery, Hedge Craft, even Kitchen Witchery, that managed to survive the Witchcraze; much of it is devoted to the healing, magical and psychotropic world-bridging powers of plants. It was handed down from generation to generation – there was no lab to provide herbal information to our ancestors. Like other shamans, they originally learned the healing power of a plant because the plant told them. Shamans listen to the spirits of all things. This is the key to working with all natural objects. Learn to listen.

Practice: Listening to plants

Work with the plants in your place of power. Ask who they are, what their purpose is, whether they need anything from you. Ask what lessons you need to learn from them. Listen for the answers.

In your magical journal, write down what you learn. Compare what you learn from the plants with what you find in a good plant book.

Science is now confirming our ancestral wisdom used to create oils and incenses, potions and baths, elixirs and formulas that healed, helped and yes, manifested magic. Peppermint perks you up while lavender relaxes you. St. John's wort improves depression, while digitalis helps a heart condition. And did you know that if a plant is poisonous or harmful, such as poison ivy, its antidote is always growing nearby?

Experience has taught us to honor what the plant world teaches us – if a plant tells you it can heal a *physically* injured heart and science proves it can, why can't a plant be right when it tells you it can heal an *emotionally* broken heart? Everything is energy and everything is interconnected – including a broken heart and the heart-healing energies of plants.

Plants we usually call herbs are used in magical potions of all sorts, like incense, bathing elixirs, magical pouches, poultices, food and offerings for all manner of goals like love, healing, prosperity, protection, peace of mind, altering and enhancing your consciousness and banishing, to name a few.

On the following page is a list of essential herbs that you can creatively combine for a wide variety of purposes. You should be able to acquire most at a local health food or even grocery store, any Wiccan shop, farmers' market, or best of all by growing them yourself. A mortar and pestle is useful for grinding and combining, and you might want to dedicate one to magical work and not making guacamole. Remember, it matters what part of the plant you use and how you use it – a leaf might be medicinal, the root deadly.

Essential herbs and their uses	
Bay leaves	Prosperity and success, banishing
Chamomile	Relaxation, purification, peace, dreams, psychic sensitivity
Cinnamon	Love and passion, banishing, prosperity and success; a pinch accelerates everything
Frankincense	Peace and protection, psychic sensitivity, God energies
Lavender	Relaxation, purification, healing, peace and protection, dreams, psychic sensitivity
Mugwort	Dreams, divination, psychic sensitivity
Myrrh	Love and passion, Goddess energies, healing, banishing
Patchouli	Love and passion, healing, purification, relaxation
Peppermint	Cleansing, energizing; a dash accelerates everything
Red pepper	A dash accelerates everything
Rose petals	Love and passion, healing
Rosemary	Relaxation and purification, peace and protection, love
Sage	Purification, healing, peace and protection, psychic sensitivity
Sandalwood	Purification, dreams, enhancing psychic sensitivities, peace
Vervain	Cleansing, relaxation, peace and protection, prosperity and success

Practice: Concocting a potion

Decide on your goal and create an herbal potion to help you. A potion in which you bathe is a wonderful way to begin mastering this kind of magic.

Wrap your potion in a handkerchief or facecloth, float it in a bathtub of warm water and immerse yourself – perhaps chanting a short spell you've written – until you see and feel your goal manifesting or whatever you need to banish washing away. Or use it to scrub yourself in the shower. Thank the element of Water and the plants when you're done.

Oils

The use of oils for healing, transformation of mood, magic and many other purposes goes back thousands of years and is an essential part of Wiccan magic. The science of scent can explain much, but then magic takes over. One of the women in my very first circle was a painter who became utterly fascinated by the mixing of oils – within a few months she was creating the most extraordinary concoctions that could cure a cold, mend a broken heart and summon a new love.

I still have the Isis oil I mixed 30 years ago – its perfume and power has become more intense over the years, contained within a crystal sphere capped with a golden bust of the Goddess Isis. It sits in a place of honor to consecrate my most precious undertakings.

You'll use oils for anointing yourself and your tools, for herbal potions and incenses (don't use too much or they won't burn), to rub onto candles for rituals and spells, and for healing, mood, energy and making magic.

Anointing your body is done with less than a drop of oil placed on each of your pulse points – at your throat, heart, underarms, crook of your arms, wrists, groin, behind your knees and ankles, and if you wish, your third eye. Or keep it simple with just a touch at your third eye, throat, heart, groin and ankles.

Aromatherapy has so popularized oils that you can find them in your local pharmacy or gift shop. Try to find organic and essential oils as there are now many faux products, but do keep in mind the importance of sustainability as the creation of oils and their sources can raise environmental issues.

Essential oils and their uses	
Almond	Love, prosperity
Bergamot	Prosperity, protection
Eucalyptus	Cleaning, purification (be careful as it's an irritant)
Frankincense	See herbs list
Jasmine	Love and sexuality, the Goddess
Lavender	See herbs list
Patchouli	See herbs list
Sandalwood	See herbs list

Crystals

An early and extraordinary lesson in the power of crystals was the effect my quartz crystal had on the dark green velvet fabric in which I had wrapped it. I used the crystal to preserve precious memories, viewing the scene through the crystal to fix the memory in my mind and within the quartz. It had been resting for several months in the drawer of a dresser, in a closet in the center of my apartment, completely hidden from the Sun or any other light source. When I finally took it out of the drawer, the green fabric was bleached red-brown.

We think of crystals as inanimate and yet they grow and are known to change in the same ways at the same moment in different locations across the globe. And computers wouldn't work without them – the world's information is stored on micro-thin slices of crystal. Like molecules of water that have been discovered to shift in response to the emotions of the person holding the water, a world of magic resides within a stone.

Crystals and stones can be worn on the body, placed on an altar, in a pouch or bundle, under a pillow or next to the bed, used as talismans or amulets or, if the spirit of your place of power agrees, in your place of power. I'm not an advocate of burying crystals – Mother Earth puts them where she wants them; and we must be mindful about the environmental and ethical issues of 'harvesting' them.

Crystals are aides, guides, spirit helpers, teachers and healers in ways that they will share with you. They help connect us to the powers of Earth, color, light and energy and seem to have a profound balancing effect on our body, mood, mind and spirit. Are the effects real or placebo? Science has not (yet) confirmed crystals' healing powers, so I would say use them to complement, not replace, traditional medical treatment.

Finding your crystal

Discovering a crystal, gem or stone to work with is a profound and magical process of discovering one of your most important power objects, actually, a Spirit ally. I thought I was finding my quartz crystal but after many years of working together, I'm sure it was calling me and leading me to it.

Cleansing it

Don't bathe it in salt water. A mild solution of chamomile or even soft soap in warm water will work well. Depending on its energy, place it outside in a safe spot and let it charge or absorb the energy of the Sun, Moon or Earth.

Establishing a relationship

Crystals with which you've established a relationship will accelerate, amplify and focus your energies, thoughts, intentions and efforts, and so you'll want to use the stone or crystal that's in natural harmony with your purpose. Just as you work with other natural objects, hold it in your hand, open your heart and mind, pay attention and listen to what it has to teach you. Write down what you learn in your magical journal.

Crystals and stones and their uses	
Amethyst	Calm and tranquility; aids sleep and dreaming; inspires happiness and positivity; relieves stress and helps break addictions
Carnelian	Encourages passion, sensuality, sexual energy, strength
Diamond	Prosperity, strength, courage, good health and solar energies
Emerald	Prosperity, intellectual capacity, psychic sensitivity; reputed to bring truth to light
Garnet	Creativity, charisma, attracts love; used as an amulet of protection for travelers
Granite	Stability, determination, balance
Hematite	Strength, calmness, peace of mind; good for blood issues and stress
Jade	Calming, encourages kindness, longevity and good fortune; attracts friendship; used as an amulet of protection for travelers
Jet	Dispels and protects against negative energies; encourages empathy, healing
Lapis lazuli	A stone of the Goddess Isis/Divine Feminine; spirituality, mysticism, wisdom, truth, integrity, abundance, wealth
Marble	Renewal, compassion, strength
Moonstone	A stone of Diana, Artemis and other Moon Goddesses; attracts lovers, enhances beauty and devotion; an amulet of protection for travelers
Obsidian	Brings truth to light; dispels negativity; peace of mind; used by Native American medicine people for healing
Opal	Creativity, prosperity, good luck and power

(continued)

Crystals and stones and their uses (continued)	
Quartz clear	Healing, cleansing of mind, body, spirit; brings truth to light; preserves magic
Quartz rose	A crystal of the Goddess Venus; love, joy, happiness, peace, harmony; often used in love spells; balances the throat chakra
Ruby	Good luck, prosperity, contentment
Sapphire	Love, partnership, protection, power, inspiration; helps with depression
Tiger's eye	Insight, integrity, overcoming obstacles
Topaz	Justice, strength, mental clarity
Turquoise	Protection, especially of the home; aligns energies and harmonizes friendships; comfort, peace; a stone of great power in Native American culture

Color

It may be difficult at first to recognize that crystals or herbs or oils are actually energy, but even people who fell asleep during art or science class know that colors are differing wavelengths of light: red, orange, yellow, green, blue, indigo and violet. Red is the longest visible color wavelength, violet the shortest.

Color is particularly useful in our creative spiritual work because each color has specific properties and effects confirmed by science. Red is the color of power and passionate love, and psychologists have discovered that people feel energized, even becoming confrontational, after spending time surrounded by red. At the other end of the spectrum, blue is the color of peace and healing and studies have shown it has precisely this effect on people.

Many people know that color is related to the seven chakras. They're also associated with the directions and deities and are a vital part of ritual, ceremony, spellcasting and all sorts of magic. For example, when you create a ritual for love or empowerment, you'll work with the color red for love and passion using a red altar cloth, candles, stones, flowers, even food and wearing red clothes. The chart below provides more useful information for working with colors in creating ceremony and making magic. The Table of Correspondences (*see pages 80–81*) also sets out colors and their spiritual associations.

Colors and their qualities		
Color	Association	Quality
Red	Fire	Passion, courage
Orange	Fire	Success, healing
Yellow	Fire	Illumination, success, healing
Green	Earth	Creativity, abundance, growth, rebirth
Blue	Water	Healing, peace, dreams, womb-resting
Indigo	Water/Spirit	Dreaming, altered states, Spirit
Purple	Spirit	Spirit, inspiration, divination
Pink	Goddess	Divine Feminine, joy
Brown	Earth	Mother Earth, soil, growth, justice
White	Spirit	Purification, Spirit, beginnings, peace
Black	Mystery	Unknown, deep rest, death, all colors
Silver	Goddess	Divine Feminine, Moon
Gold	God	Divine Masculine, Sun

Creating power objects

Natural objects can become objects of power for various purposes, based on their innate gifts and their willingness to work with you, and also by 'charging' them for a specific purpose. 'Charging' means infusing an object with intention, purpose and energy (see below).

You can also create a power object. Like everything else, all power objects and their parts come originally from Nature, like a branch used as a wand, a shell used as a cup, a metal knife or pentacle forged from the elements with a handle carved from wood, a drum with the head made from an animal skin and the frame from a tree, or a crystal-tipped wand of willow charged with the memories and energies of all your rituals done beneath the Moon.

A power object can be anything that calls or speaks to you, inviting you to work with it for a specific purpose. Power objects can be found, purchased or crafted and then charged with power to give them a specific purpose, such as healing or divination or as an offering.

Talismans and amulets are venerable power objects created for a wide range of magical purposes, and there's a vast realm of symbolism and lore associated with them. They are also utterly simple and natural – a piece of parchment on which you've written your spell or simply a symbol of it, a crystal worn about your neck charged with magical purpose, a pouch of green fabric tied with golden thread in which you've placed a large silver coin and a potion of bay leaves, basil, cinnamon and sugar.

Practice: Charging a power object

1. Cleanse and purify your object

This can be done simply by washing it in water and salt (except for crystals and silver, which can be damaged) or chamomile or soft, organic soap, or by burying it in the Earth for 24 hours, or moving it through the purifying smoke of an herb like sage.

2. Charge your object

This can be done quite simply. Before you begin, consider which element the object is related to, as you'll draw on that power to charge it. Cast a circle, place your cleansed object on the altar and state your intention and the purpose and power for which the object will be charged.

Thank the object for lending itself, its power and wisdom to you. Call the aid of deity, Spirit or element to assist you, holding the object in both hands and against your heart. Breathe into it and hold it aloft to charge it with the powers of Air and then to your third eye; hold it above a flame for Fire and then to your stomach for a Fire object; place it in or sprinkle it with Water to charge it with the powers of Water and touch it to your heart; and ground and run the energies of the Earth through yourself and into an Earth object, and touch it to the Earth.

You can also charge your object with a combination of all of the elements or with the power of the Sun or Moon by placing it under their light, or the Earth by burying it for 24 hours. Then hold the object against your heart (again), directing your energies, intentions and appreciation into the object. Feel it absorbing your energy – you should experience a sense of warmth, tingling and communion.

If you wish, you may say: *'I call upon the divine power within this (object) to awaken. I charge this (object) with the divine power that dwells within me, I charge you with the element of _____, with the blessings of Goddess, God and Oneness. Bless me with your (name a gift or power of the object), with your gifts known and unknown, and aid me as I become whole, wise and fully alive.'*

Thank Spirit, Mother Earth and the object for helping you.

If it's a Goddess object or tool, like a chalice, you might want to fill it with water or wine and leave it beneath the full Moon for the night. If it's a God object or tool, like an athame (see below) you might want to leave it beneath the Sun for a day. Return it to your altar or carefully wrap it and keep it somewhere safe and private until you're ready to work with it. And always greet it with respect when you work with it.

Wiccan tools of art

'Tools of art' or 'working tools' are traditional Wiccan power objects. They have their origins in ceremonial magical traditions, and although it's unlikely that a *wicce* owned and used a magical sword, the natural elements and aspects of divinity that tools of art symbolize date back to the early Greeks as well as shamanic traditions. They are also connected to the pre-Christian Mysteries of the Holy Grail.

You don't need them to practice, but more than just symbols of the elements and deity, they can be powerful and empowering to work with.

The traditional tools of art include the following:

❖ An athame (pronounced a' tham ee): a double-sided knife, often with a black handle

❖ A wand

❖ A (silver) cup

❖ A (copper or stone) pentacle: round, flat and carved or marked with a five-pointed star

Along with these four, you'll want a 'white hilt knife,' for carving candles, digging wax out of candlesticks and cutting all sorts of things from ribbons to thread to fruit – it can be a small kitchen knife with any handle.

Tools of art			
Tool	Purpose	Element	Symbol
Wand	Directing energy	Air or Fire	God, Mind, Will
Cup	Holding energy, liquids	Water	Goddess, Heart, Womb
Athame/sword	Directing energy	Air or Fire	God, Mind, Will
Pentacle	Charging and consecrating	Earth, Spirit	Goddess and God, Lover and Beloved, body, four elements, directions and Spirit

Other essential tools include a brazier or other fireproof container for burning incense for the element Air, a candle and candlestick for Fire, a small bowl or large shell to hold Water, another small bowl to hold the element Earth, usually as salt or seeds, a large (usually silver) bowl, chalice or cup for libations and offerings and a small cauldron for magic, both symbolizing the Goddess, a drum and a rattle. See the diagram of a traditional Wiccan altar in Chapter 6, which shows where these tools are positioned.

Gradually, you may also accumulate statues, altar cloths of different colors, a staff, perhaps a sword, talismans, amulets, jewelry, tools of divination, and create a magical pouch (a 'medicine bundle' in Native American traditions).

Your magical journal and/or Book of Shadows, which we'll discuss in Chapter 12, is a power object, as well as your altar. Just remember, less is often more. You don't need any of these to make magic or cast spells, though they will certainly help you when you do use them. You'll also go through stages where you'll neither need nor want to work with power objects, or prefer only a few. When you do return to using them, you'll do so with greater appreciation of their aesthetic and other powers.

A quick note on etiquette: Never pick up someone else's working tools without first asking their permission.

The Wiccan Altar

The altar is where your tools and power objects reside when you make magic. Generally placed in the center of your circle, it can also sit in the direction that best corresponds to the work you're doing: for example, in the North if you're working for prosperity. Your altar can be set up each time you work, or permanently, and should then receive your daily devotion, even if that's just a moment of acknowledgment and dusting. Above all, your altar should remind you that *you* are the altar where Spirit and form are One. See Chapter 6 for layout and more information.

Where Spirit and Earth are One

As his or her adventure begins, every hero is given a magical tool – Dorothy's ruby slippers, Luke's light saber, Harry's wand. It serves, protects and empowers them as they venture forth in realms of challenge and magic. Tools and talismans, power objects and potions are eloquent teachers of *how* the Divine is embodied in the material world – and in *you*.

But no object can make magic *for* you; they will, however, make magic *with* you. They are conductors of divinity and when used over a long period, power objects develop a deep relationship with you and tremendous power. Ultimately, all heroes learn what you will learn – the magic is inside *you*. It originates from the divinity awakened within you, as you work reverently and consciously with the divinity awakened within your ingredients, power objects and tools.

Chapter 12

The Adventure Ahead

We are a circle, within a circle, with no beginning, and never ending...

Ahead of you lies a spiritual adventure beyond anything you first imagined. Wherever you choose to go next, whatever challenge confronts you, whatever Mystery beckons, you have everything you need for your journey.

You have the power to re-enchant your life, and the world.

Cultivating personal practice

Personal practice is one of the keys to awakening the magic within you *and* in the world that embraces you. It's as simple as a daily act that connects you to the Sacred – a practice or action that opens your heart, keeps you present in your body and in the positive feelings of the moment; something that helps you pay attention and experience your connection to the natural world, its divinity and its blessings.

You can perform a daily meditation at your altar, water the plants growing on your windowsill or feed the birds in your yard. You can act in accord with the spell you've cast, reread yesterday's journal entry, or take your dog for a walk and pay attention to what she pays attention to.

It doesn't have to take long – just a few minutes is enough to experience the rush of energy, the mindfulness and gratitude that awaken magic. It's how I start my day, and it's a wonderful way to end the day. Whatever you choose, daily, personal ritual is magical.

Wonderful as living with this awakened magical sensibility is, it can also be challenging. Divine magic disrupts, disorients and disconnects you from the things that stand between you and your sacred self. Past patterns get challenged, self-doubt rises to the surface, the dreams we once held dear are no longer meaningful. And sometimes, the new dreams that we put our heart and soul into, for which we craft the most compelling spells, fail to manifest. Sometimes the magic just doesn't seem to work and the Sacred seems to have forgotten us. What then?

Divination

You're never alone. You may forget, or doubt, or find yourself in a winter cycle of silence and stillness, but there's one practice in particular that will always connect you to the Divine – divination.

Divination is not just a way of predicting the future. Its real purpose is found within the word itself: divination is a way for you to engage in a dialogue with divinity, to receive the guidance, insights and inspiration that you need in daily life and on your soul's great adventure.

Divination is a prayer that's always answered. It's an act of communion, an experience of love and wisdom the Divine offers you. Reliably, your inner magic awakens when you realize the Divine is aware of you and present when you need help.

More than seeing the future

There's another gift that divination offers you: a mirror to see deeply within, to know yourself – your strengths as well as shadows. Any method of divination is an oracle, which actually means the mouth or voice of divinity. It's the Divine guiding you to find the gold within the darkness.

Divination reveals your soul's true purpose. It helps you understand the deep meanings within the events of your life – good and bad – and so helps you transform loss, longing or difficulties into wisdom, empowerment and fulfillment.

Divination actually teaches you that the future is *not* predestined. When you try to see into the future, divination shows the *probability* of where you'll end up, based on how you are feeling, believing and behaving *now*. It shows possibilities, not inevitabilities.

With the divine guidance an oracle provides, we can understand ourselves, our learned patterns and unconscious impulses, the meaning of a current situation, relationship or dilemma. The insights divination provides can help us to change how we feel, think and behave, and so change our future. If there is indeed a destiny, it's the one that divination liberates you to fulfill.

On the path into realms of magic where wonder dwells and where you'll also be tested, divination is a sacred GPS. It helps you know where you're headed and how to get there. And, working with divination, you're also cultivating your intuition and your confidence. Best of all, every time you use divination, you're being guided by the Sacred: you are *never* alone.

Practical advice for divination

There are countless methods that enable you to send and receive a message, almost all of which rely on a symbol system rooted in Nature – whether it's astrology, Tarot or oracle cards, runes, the I Ching, or directly reading signs in Nature. In fact, the Divine will use whatever is at hand to communicate with you, whether it's a synchronicity, a *cledon* (the ancient Greek term for a spontaneous sacred message), a dream or many other methods. You just have to pay attention.

Finding your first divination tool isn't complicated – just allow your intuition to guide you to whatever feels most appealing. Buy, find or create it, purify it, cultivate your relationship with it, sleep with it beneath your pillow for one lunar cycle and then consecrate it as you would any magical tool. And begin working with it. Address it with respect and gratitude. It *is* an oracle, the voice of the Sacred.

One of the simplest and most useful daily practices is to begin or end the day with a simple question and a simple divination. It will help you to understand the purpose and the wisdom within any situation. And it enables you to use the insight it gives you to transform any challenge into empowerment. Daily divination will also cultivate your intuition, your self-knowledge and confidence, and along the way you'll master a language and system of divination and cultivate your relationship with the Divine. It's a wonderful practice.

Practice: Daily divination

Every morning, take a moment to breathe, ground and clear your heart and mind. Then hold your divination tool to your heart and ask one simple question, like: *'What do I need to know to have the best day possible?'*

♦ Pull a single Tarot or oracle card, rune or I Ching hexagram, etc. Study it, allowing the image itself to speak to you, allowing your imagination and intuition to 'see.' Then look up the meaning in the guide/interpretation book that comes with your tool. Write down the symbol and the meaning – a few key words should be enough.

♦ Use another one of my favorite methods – ask the help of the Library Angel as you randomly open a book and allow your eyes to land on a sentence. Or directly 'read' the signs in Nature, paying careful attention to the appearance of an animal, a feather in your path, the shape of clouds, the whispering of trees.

♦ Put the expression, image, symbol or sentence where you can see it during the day. As the events of the day play out, consider the advice you were given. At the end of the day, revisit the message and write about its meaning and how it helped your day.

The Divine also guides you with synchronicities and epiphanies that reveal the Sacred Mysteries of *your* life. Divination helps you to recognize and understand their meaning and the heroic journey that is uniquely yours.

Creating personal ritual

An easy, simple, personal act repeated regularly becomes a ritual and can be your daily practice. You can also cast circle and make magic in weekly, monthly or seasonal rites where you awaken and honor the divine magic within you and that surrounds you.

In addition to the rites that celebrate the cycles of seasons, Sun, Earth and Moon, life is full of crossroads and events that deserve and require rituals. They are the passages that profoundly change who you are and who you'll become. Some are undertaken voluntarily, others come by force of time or unexpected tragedy, triumph or destiny. We grow up, friendships and love affairs begin and end, we get married and divorced, end pregnancies and give birth to children or dreams, achieve a great goal, break a bad habit, change careers, come out of the closet or go live in the woods. Loved ones die, we age and accidents or illness change our course and deepen the meaning of our lives.

Life provides endless opportunities to discover and fulfill the magic of who you are, and who you're meant to be, and ritual is part of the process of discovering, becoming and celebrating. This book provides you with all the skills and information, and I hope encouragement, to create rituals to honor all the magical moments and turning points in your life, whether difficult or blissful.

And remember, rituals and magic are not just for the momentous. They are also for the simple matters of daily life, whether it's setting your intention as the day begins or releasing stress as the day ends, finding solace or inspiration to make a difficult decision or getting the energy to accomplish your goals. Personal rituals are precious time for self-care, reflection and raising energy that you need and deserve. Whatever the occasion, great or small, creating personal rituals will fill your life with magic.

Wiccan rituals can also be group celebrations: creating beautiful, meaningful and helpful rites of passage is something you can do for others. It's a gift we can give to honor, support and assist the ones we love, to deepen friendships and create caring communities grounded in the sacredness of our shared life. Rituals have the power to transform lives and to transform the world.

Two examples in which I've often participated were once disempowering taboos – a girl's first menstruation and a woman's passage through menopause – both now increasingly honored by women alone and in circles with rituals of empowerment and sisterhood. And young men and old, transgender and gender non-specific, are increasingly creating rituals of personal meaning as well.

Practice: Creating a personal ritual

Reflect on an event in your life that should be ritualized. What's the purpose of your ritual, the meaning of the event you're going to honor, the meaning of the event in your life?

❖   Use divination to help you more fully understand yourself and the deeper meaning of this event in the story of your life. Consider how it reflects the great cycles of Nature and determine when the natural cycles of Earth, Sun or Moon coincide with your ritual's goal.

❖   Determine if you want to work with a specific deity, spirit being or element. Consider which would be most beneficial to your purpose and ways of working with them. Use the Table of Correspondences to determine which deities, colors, herbs and plants, symbols and images to work with in creating your ritual. Use your intuition and creativity.

❖   Create an altar that reflects the energies, deities, spirits and elements with which you'll work.

❖   Create an object, talisman, amulet, work of art, poem or offering that symbolizes and expresses the goal or purpose of your ritual.

❖   Write your invocation of the four directions and the elements, addressing the relationship between the elements and your goal.

❖   Write your invocation of deity, connecting their blessings and transformative powers to the goal of your ritual.

❖   Cast your circle and work creatively with the invocations, techniques and information you've learned to express your ritual's purpose.

❖   Make your magic – honor yourself or whomever the rite is for. Leave room for spontaneity and divinity. Make your offering and express your gratitude for the change this ritual marks. Honor the way in which your life is your magic.

❖   Close your circle. Reflect and write about it in your magical journal.

Creating your own Book of Shadows

A Book of Shadows is a written collection of Wiccan invocations, blessings, rituals, expressions of gratitude and wisdom. You can also create a *grimoire*, a companion book of spells, recipes, formulas, symbolic alphabets, magical lore and workings and more wisdom.

Keeping a Book of Shadows is a modern practice. Early Wicca was an Indigenous shamanic wisdom tradition and so it was mostly an oral tradition. And later, even if you could read, you certainly wouldn't keep evidence of your religion in the midst of deadly persecutions.

But in the mid-20th century, Gerald Gardner, the father of modern Wicca, began keeping a book of wisdom that he called a Book of Shadows. He and High Priestess Doreen Valiente created and preserved a coherent system of sacred rites that was passed on to initiates in the Gardnerian tradition's Book of Shadows. The initiate was supposed to hand-copy the original, which never left the possession of the Priestess.

Today you don't need to be initiated in a tradition to create your own Book of Shadows. It's an ongoing spiritual creation, preserving the invocations and rituals, spells and practices that you've found meaningful, evocative and effective. Your Book of Shadows is also meant to be filled with beauty: whether you're an artist or not, adding images, pressed flowers, even doodles and other ornamentation is not just OK, it's gorgeous.

While a Book of Shadows has a traditional structure and content, you may also want to include important dreams, readings and results of divinations, chants and songs, poetry and inspiring prose, wisdom received from your guides and power animals, from Drawing Down or journeying and other sources. You may also wish to preserve these in journals, diaries or a *grimoire*.

When I began, I kept my journals in spiral-bound notebooks and used beautiful blank books covered in tooled leather or printed silk for my Books of Shadow. Yes, *books* plural because if you continue to practice Wicca, you'll collect an extraordinary amount of wisdom and beauty.

This book has provided you with basic texts that you can read and memorize and, if you wish, copy into your own Book of Shadows. Over time, you'll expand your repertoire, drawing on other sources including, most importantly, your own creativity. And things will come to you spontaneously, especially in Nature. Whenever possible, as soon as you're done, write down what you did and said and experienced so you don't forget it. Your Book of Shadows is one of your most beautiful power objects, so keep it some place safe and treat it with the love and respect it, and you, deserve.

Enjoy!

Essential content of your Book of Shadows

1. Title page: 'This is the Book of Shadows of -----
(your name)'

2. Dedication page: this is a simple statement from your heart about what you hope for your spiritual journey on the path of Wicca. Reflect on what has drawn you to this moment of awakening. If you wish to cast a spell on the book, this is the place for it. Write the date and astrological aspect and sign it.

3. *The Charge of the Goddess*: every Book of Shadows includes this Goddess invocation (*see page 124*). You may also wish to add your own or other invocations of the Goddess or Goddesses.

4. Invocation of the God: as with the Goddess above

5. A diagram of your altar: this is very helpful if you are passing on your Book.

6. Markings for your working tools. This is very old school: charging runes and other markings were typically painted or carved on handles, etc. Read more about this on my website, www.phylliscurott.com

7. Purification: of Self, circle

8. Breathing meditation

9. Grounding and centering

10. Casting Circle/Creating Sacred Space

11. Honoring the Four Directions

12. Invocation of Divinity/Goddess/God

13. Texts of rituals; blessings; chants, songs of power; journeys of magical significance; divinations; meditations; visualizations; magic; energy working; dance steps; spells, although some people prefer to keep these in their *grimoire*.

14. Libations and expressions of received wisdom

15. Expressions and offerings of gratitude

16. Thanking and closing the four directions

17. Closing and releasing circle

18. Esbats – waxing, full, waning, dark Moon rites; invocations to Draw Down the Moon

19. Sabbats – rituals for each of the eight holy days in the Wheel of the Year

20. Ritual of self-dedication (see below)

21. Initiation ritual

Creating your *grimoire*

You may also want to keep a *grimoire*. This is the fun and crafty aspect of the Craft of the Wise that we explored in Chapter 11. It's also the divinely embodied artistry of Wicca. A *grimoire* includes everything that engages all of your senses, alters your consciousness and helps you shape and direct your energies – transforming the mundane into the magical. A great deal of this information is provided within the pages of this book, and of course, you'll find other resources elsewhere – just be sure to check the expertise of the source.

It's all the elements of Green Magic – working with herbs, oils, potions, recipes and formulas. It's Creative Magic – working with chants, dances, poetry, movement, language and more. It's Traditional Magic – working with symbolism, tools, talismans, amulets, sigils and more.

Essential content of your grimoire

1. Title page (see Book of Shadows)

2. Dedication page (see Book of Shadows)

3. Information about deities

4. Information about the elements, Nature

5. Information about the natural environment of your home

6. Tools of art – list each tool, draw a picture of it, describe its magical purpose and connection to the elements, and its symbolism

7. Magical information:

   » Table of Correspondences

   » Chants, dances, songs, prayers, spells, words of wisdom, quotes from others

   » Wisdom and insights you've received during ritual, meditation, journeys, etc.

» Potions

» Incenses

» Symbols and magical alphabets

» Divination – describe the divination tools you're working with, draw their symbols and describe their meanings. This can include runes (draw the rune and write down its meaning and interpretation), Tarot cards, astrological signs, your astrological chart.

» Important divinatory readings

» Spells

» Talismans

» Sigils

» Signs

» Information about herbs, oils, gems, candles, crystals

» Methods of working magic, such as elemental, trance work, knot magic, scrying and others – you can learn more about these on my website, www.phylliscurott.com

Full circle

It's time to look back to the beginning of your quest: Open your magical journal and read the first pages in which you described what you were seeking. Read your reflections, impressions and descriptions of your experiences. Consider how much you've changed and achieved, all you've learned about Wicca, about magic and about yourself.

Perhaps one of the most important rituals you can create is one that marks your spiritual commitment to yourself, to Mother Earth, to the Divine. It's a rite that looks back to honor how far you've come and how much you've changed. It's a rite that looks forward as you make a commitment to yourself and to the path that lies ahead.

It's a ritual of rejoicing and honoring who you are, in this moment, in this place, in your life, your body, your spirit. It's a rite that honors and awakens the divine magic within you. And if you wish, it's a rite in which you commit yourself to continuing to practice Wicca. We call it a ritual of self-dedication and below is a simple script you can use with additions only you can write. Feel free to adapt it as you wish.

Practice: Ritual of self-dedication

Take your time to read and reflect on the rite below and/or to write your own rite; when you feel you have your final draft, write it in your Book of Shadows.

1. Organize all of the items you'll need for your rite; charge Water in your chalice or Goddess bowl beneath a full Moon to use in your

rite; charge a candle on your pentacle beneath the Sun to use in your rite.

2. When the time has come to perform your self-dedication, and when the Moon and Sun are waxing to fullness, purify.

3. Write your oath: a simple commitment to yourself, to your spiritual growth, to living your life fully, courageously and with devotion to Mother Earth and the Spirit she embodies and the Spirit *you* embody. Write from your heart.

4. Create your offering. Prepare you place of power, inside or out.

5. Create your altar with symbols of your journey: include your magical journal, the tools and power objects you've created and collected, symbols of your patron deity, power animal, spirit guides, your oracle/divination tool(s), the Moon Water and Sun candle, your Goddess bowl or chalice. Your altar should most deeply express the heart and spirit of your devotion to your spiritual journey. You can also perform this rite without an altar, tools or symbols – just yourself.

6. Have your chalice and your Book of Shadows with you. Place your athame or wand on the ground as a threshold to your place of power, where your circle's perimeter will be. Sit 'outside,' in front of your athame or wand.

7. On a piece of paper, write down the parts of yourself of your past that you wish to release, surrender, banish. Burn the paper.

8. Pay attention to the shift in energies that has already begun. Reflect on your gifts, your goals, your path, where you started, how far you've come and where you wish to go. Breathe, ground and meditate using a single word, image or phrase that expresses the path ahead.

9. When you're ready, open your eyes and stand up. Say:

    *'I am ready to dedicate myself to my true and sacred
    self and to this path that lies ahead. I come to my
    future with perfect love and perfect trust.'*

10. Hold your Book of Shadows and chalice and step over your
    athame/wand. Allow yourself to fully experience crossing the
    threshold into your future. Feel your energy shift, feel the divine
    energy into which you've stepped, feel your heart open. Pick up
    your athame/wand and place your Book of Shadows and chalice
    in the center of your sacred space/altar.

11. Cast your circle. Ground, center and call upon the Goddess
    and the God, the Beloved and Lover, upon all that is divine
    surrounding and arising from within you. You may wish to say:

    *'Great Mother Goddess, by flower and by fruit I invoke
    you. Great Father God, by hoof and by horn I invoke you.
    Beneath the Moon and the Sun, standing upon Mother Earth,
    surrounded by the blessings of the Green Man, and all the
    children of Creation, I welcome you to this sacred space,
    to the temple of my heart. Embrace me and transform me.
    Bless me and fill me with your presence. Accept my offering
    as I dedicate myself to a path of beauty, wisdom and love.'*

12. Pour the Moon Water into the chalice and light the Sun candle.
    Feel the energy flowing through you. Take all the time you want
    and need. Feel the blessings of joy, peace and love. Feel the
    energies of Earth and Spirit flowing through you, merging within
    you, consecrating and transforming, nourishing and blessing you.
    Feel yourself coming home to your true self, to your destiny and
    to the Sacred. When you're ready, read your oath.

13. If you're dedicating yourself to the Wiccan path, you should add:

    'I open my eyes, my heart and my soul to the Mystery of the Sacred, everywhere present in the world and in my life. I will draw my power from the Divine and awaken to the magic of Creation, and I will always give thanks for its blessings.'

14. Consecrate yourself with the Moon Water in your chalice by placing a drop on your third eye, heart and groin, saying:

    'With the Waters of life, I bless and dedicate myself.'

15. Consecrate yourself with the Sun candle by passing the light in front of your third eye, heart and groin, saying:

    'With the Fires of life, I bless and dedicate myself.'

16. Feel yourself filled and surrounded with love, and feel love flowing from you to the world and the Sacred. Hold your Book of Shadows to your heart and charge it. Charge your jewelry or a power object that honors this rite of passage.

17. Make your offering and offer a libation to the Goddess, the God, Lover and Beloved, Earth and Spirit, and yourself where all are conjoined. Thank Creation for blessing you and for accepting your oath of dedication. Declare:

    'I am awake to the divine magic within me.'

18. Close your circle. If you're outside, as always, leave an offering for your fellow creatures in the sacred space. You may wish to keep the offering you made to honor this rite among your sacred tools and power objects. Go forth into your new life, acting in accord.

The world that you re-enter will be an enchanted one, for you have awakened to the magic within you and all around you.

My blessing for you

Even though we've not (yet) met in person, I created this book aware of your presence, as if you were standing over my shoulder reading as I wrote, working next to me as I refined each practice, sharing the experiences as if we were sitting in circle together. Because, really, we *are* in circle together.

Like seeing a new star in the night sky, I've felt the magic within you awaken. And now you know that the first thing magic changes is *you*. You're becoming wise and life will become increasingly enchanted. It's like seeing the world in color after a lifetime of black and white, like hearing someone you love say 'I love you,' after being deaf. You've awakened the most important sense of all – your sense of the Sacred. And that's where all the magic comes from.

It's a good way to live. It can also be difficult because your heart is now wide open in a world that denies the divinity of life on Earth. But if you've learned anything from this little book it's that you are *never* alone – the Divine is *always* with you. If you forget, if the world seems darkly overwhelming or the magic seems to have disappeared, use any practice from within these pages and reconnect.

And remember, there is a reason you were born in this place at this time of challenges to the future of life on Earth.

I hope our journey together has been all and more than you expected, that I have been a helpful guide, and that this book will continue to awaken and nourish your divine magic. May all your spells be charged with love and all your magic be divine. It's hard to say goodbye and so instead I'll simply say:

> *'Thou art God/dess.*
>
> *Our circle is open, but never broken.*
>
> *Merry meet and merry part and merry meet again.'*

Resources

If you'd like to continue to learn and work with me, join my mailing list. This provides first notice of special opportunities, including early registrations, exclusive private sessions and the latest news. As my gift to you, you'll also receive Weekly Words of Wisdom when you sign up at www.phylliscurott.com

I'm also active on social media and you can connect with me here:

Facebook: www.facebook.com/phylliscurott

Twitter: @phylliscurott

Goodreads: www.goodreads.com/phylliscurott

Further reading
You may also like to read my other books:

Book of Shadows, A Modern Woman's Journey into the Wisdom of Witchcraft and the Magic of the Goddess (20th anniversary edition), Fourth Rune Books, 2018)

WitchCrafting, A Spiritual Guide to Making Magic, Broadway Books/Random House (2002)

The Love Spell, An Erotic Memoir of Spiritual Awakening, Gotham Books/Penguin (2004)

You might also enjoy my YouTube video, 'How to Set Up a Wiccan Altar': https://www.youtube.com /watch?v=2jlgy4mhijl&t=8s

ABOUT THE AUTHOR

Joseph Ferlise

Phyllis Curott is one of America's first public Wiccan Priestesses, an attorney and author whose groundbreaking books have made Wicca accessible to the world and awakened an entire generation to the Goddess. Widely covered in the international media, she was inducted into the Martin Luther King Jr. Collegium of Clergy and Scholars, is Vice Chair Emerita of the 2015 Parliament of the World's Religions, and founder of the Temple of Ara.

Curott received her degree in philosophy from Brown University and her Juris Doctor from New York University.

 phylliscurott

 @phylliscurott

www.phylliscurott.com
www.templeofara.net

Hay House Podcasts
Bring Fresh, Free Inspiration Each Week!

Hay House proudly offers a selection of life-changing audio content via our most popular podcasts!

Hay House Meditations Podcast

Features your favorite Hay House authors guiding you through meditations designed to help you relax and rejuvenate. Take their words into your soul and cruise through the week!

Dr. Wayne W. Dyer Podcast

Discover the timeless wisdom of Dr. Wayne W. Dyer, world-renowned spiritual teacher and affectionately known as "the father of motivation." Each week brings some of the best selections from the 10-year span of Dr. Dyer's talk show on Hay House Radio.

Hay House Podcast

Enjoy a selection of insightful and inspiring lectures from Hay House Live events, listen to some of the best moments from previous Hay House Radio episodes, and tune in for exclusive interviews and behind-the-scenes audio segments featuring leading experts in the fields of alternative health, self-development, intuitive medicine, success, and more! Get motivated to live your best life possible by subscribing to the free Hay House Podcast.

Find Hay House podcasts on iTunes, or visit www.HayHouse.com/podcasts for more info.

HAY HOUSE

Look within

Join the conversation about latest products,
events, exclusive offers and more.

f   Hay House UK

🐦   @HayHouseUK

📷   @hayhouseuk

❤   healyourlife.com

We'd love to hear from you!